STREAMS OF GRACE

RICHARD R. NIEBUHR
Florence Corliss Lamont Professor of Divinity
Harvard Divinity School

WIPF & STOCK · Eugene, Oregon

Wipf and Stock Publishers
199 W 8th Ave, Suite 3
Eugene, OR 97401

Streams of Grace
Studies of Jonathan Edwards, Samuel Taylor Coleridge
and William James
By Niebuhr, Richard R.
Copyright©1980 by Niebuhr, Richard R.
ISBN 13: 978-1-61097-042-6
Publication date 10/13/2010
Previously published by Doshisha University Press, 1980

CONTENTS

Preface	i
Introduction	1
"Living Symbols" : A Chapel Talk	6
"Being Is Proportion": Jonathan Edwards' Philosophy of Excellency	12
"Know Thyself!": Samuel Taylor Coleridge's Science of Living Words	39
William James' Metaphysics of Religious Experience	76
"The Generous Eye" : A Sermon	115

Every bit of us at every moment is part and parcel of a wider self, it quivers along various radii like the wind-rose on a compass, and the actual in it is continuously one with possibles not yet in our present sight.

William James

PREFACE

THE visit that my wife, Nancy, and I enjoyed as the guests of Doshisha University in the month of May 1980 lives in our memories with an intensity and accompanying sense of pleasure and gratitude that no other period of time we have spent abroad even begins to rival. The visit was made possible by the invitation Chancellor Naozo Ueno and the faculties of Doshisha extended to me to give the second Neesima Memorial Lectures. When this generous invitation arrived, I eagerly accepted it. I had for some months been slowly projecting plans to visit Japan for a brief time, partly to follow the route of the poet-traveller, Matsuo Bashō, through "the far north," for I had become fascinated by this extraordinary pilgrim and his "travel diary." But at that time I had on notion of the riches of hospitality and cordial friendliness that awaited us at Doshisha nor of the beauty of the city of Kyoto we were to discover.

Since our return from Japan the work of polishing the lectures I delivered has been interrupted by a number of claims upon me that I could not turn aside. As the weeks grew into months and the revisions I originally intended remained incomplete, I found it necessary to do more re-thinking and re-writing than I at first anticipated, partly because the subject matter of these lectures has been and continues to be very much at the center of my attention, never ceasing to open to me new insights and connections; and partly because as time passed I found myself increasingly wanting to send back to our hosts at Doshisha as finished a piece of work as I could manage.

Accordingly, the first lecture, on Jonathan Edwards, has been re-written with a view to making it clearer; the second lecture, on Samuel Taylor Coleridge, has been entirely recast and bears little resemblance to the manuscript from which I read in May of 1980. The third lecture, on William James, has also been re-worked and expanded, though it is not substantively different from the draft I carried with me to Kyoto nearly two years ago. Finally, I have added a preface, identifying several of the themes and ideas that run throughout the lectures as a whole.

There are so many indviduals at Doshisha to whom I am indebted, that a list of their names would begin to resemble a list of the Faculties of Theology and of Letters. I must record my gratitude, however, to the persons who translated my chapel talk and lectures as I delivered them, Professor Masao Takenaka of the Faculty of Theology, Associate Professor Takashi Sasaki of the Center for American Studies, Professor Muneharu Kitagaki of the Faculty of Letters, Professor Nobuyuki Oda of the Women's College, and Professor Robert Fukada of the Faculty of Theology. These men and their colleagues extended to my wife and to myself countless other courtesies as well. Indeed, to remember all the kindnesses we received is to be overwhelmed again. Nor am I likely ever to forget the afternoon Professor Susumu Kamaike took us to see Bashō's favorite abode in the Kyoto area, the Rakushisha, and the visit Professor Osamu Takayama made possible for us in the home of his remarkable father, the noted ceramicist. My wife and I still dream of the lovely *Muhinshuan* at Amherst House, which Professor Otis Cary graciously opened to us as our cottage for the month. None of this would have come about except for Masao Takenaka, whom we had the good fortune to come to know years ago at Yale, and my particular thanks goes to him and to his wife.

Here in Greater Boston I am grateful to the trustees of the Marion and Jasper Whiting Foundation, who gave me a grant to carry out my explorations of Bashō's route and become initially acquainted with Japan. Here at Harvard I am grateful to Ms. Evelyn Rosenthal of the Divinity School for her patient typing and retyping of the manuscript and the seemingly infinite revisions I have made in it. My friend, Carol Zaleski, took time from her own writing about other-worldly journeys to make the charming graphic of the spider-web that enhances the lecture on Jonathan Edwards.

The Divinity School
Harvard University
August 1983

INTRODUCTION

JONATHAN Edwards (1703-1758), the New England preacher and theologian, Samuel Taylor Coleridge (1772-1834), the English poet and critic, and William James (1842-1910), the American psychologist and formative interpreter of pragmatism are ordinarily counted not merely as men of diverse accomplishments but as citizens of diverse worlds: of declining American Puritanism, of flourishing English-German romanticism, and of American post-Civil War nationalism and optimism. Each of them gave much of his life to philosophy, but we do not spontaneously think of them as making up a natural subset within western, Euro-American intellectual culture generally or within the development of its religious thought in particular. Yet these three shared certain large convictions—convictions apparently resilient in significant social and political change—which are important, I believe, to all who care for philosophy of religion or for philosophy in religion or for the reason religion generates out of its own reflecting nature. And they set these convictions out, furthermore, in such provocative ways as to have drawn me, at any rate, to return to them repeatedly over a span of years for the kind of sustained conversation and enlightenment that only wise, original, and intrepid writing can provide.

They shared, for example, the conviction that we have intellectual commerce not merely with our own thoughts and feelings but with being, with that which has the "property of *Outness*," as Coleridge liked to say.[1] Edwards used other language but to the same very general effect, when he noted: "Idea. All sorts of ideas of things

1

are but the repetitions of those very things over again—as well the ideas of colors, figures, solidity, tastes, and smells, as the ideas of thought and mental acts."[2] And James referred to our moral and intellectual acts as "the workshop of being, where we catch fact in the making."[3] All three regarded intellect not only as moving on the surfaces of appearances but as participating in the deeper currents of the real. At the root of consciousness, Coleridge wrote in his "Essay on Faith," lies conscience, and the first act of conscience coming to consciousness is to take on itself an allegiance, "a fidelity . . . to being generally."[4]

A second principle governing these authors is the principle first clearly enunciated by John Locke that all of our knowledge is founded upon and derives itself from experience: the experience provided by the senses and the experience provided by our perceptions of the operations of the mind itself. Edwards, Coleridge, and James were empiricists; they were also more than what the term empiricist commonly suggests, but they never abandoned Locke's fundamental precept. Hence, they agreed that intelligential beings must employ all "signs" scrupulously and honestly, with the utmost regard for the experience in which our mental processes initiate and grow. "Signs" stands here as the general term for words as names, as signifiers, with which we discourse about, i.e., run rapidly over, the ideas and beliefs that the variegated richness of our life's experience has yielded us; but too often we discourse or hasten from "sign" to "sign" without returning to our originary experience itself, without returning from the name to the named, to ascertain afresh the veracity and validity or strength of what we profess. Such habits turn religion "into a science of shadows under the name of theology," Coleridge warned, and he advised his readers to cultivate the science of "living words," that is, the knowledge of $\lambda\sigma\gamma o\iota$, "words" that shape and actuate the system of life to which they belong.

It is common enough to identify Edwards and James as heirs of Locke; it is uncommon so to identify Coleridge, because he renounced the philosophy—with which he was once so enamored—of David Hartley, a now forgotten expositor of Locke's theiories of the association of ideas. But his own essential tenets—that perception is the primary form of imagination; that freshness of sensation is the health of the soul; that experience is the test of all doctrine—no doubt owe much to these British philosophical progenitors.

Edwards and Coleridge were acute observers of nature with strong interests in the natural sciences. All three of these men excelled in the "perception of the operations of our own minds." This "empiricism" combined with their metaphysical bent no doubt contributed much to the third shared conviction I shall mention here, namely, that knowledge is creative action and is therefore an activity for which we must assume moral and ultimately religious responsibility. It is an action of crossing the barrier reefs of custom (the "prejudices of the imagination," as Edwards put it), of voyaging through the mists of conventional half-truths and the catch words of the day, and of venturing toward an intuited open expanse of being. The philosophies of knowledge and of being with which Edwards, Coleridge, and James worked exhibit profound differences. Nevertheless, Edwards and

Coleridge would have well understood the question James asked when he wrote: "May not you and I be confluent in a higher consciousness, and confluently active there, tho we now know it not?"[5] The kind of in quiry James' question invites is something that no mere spectator will undertake. It enagages the whole human intellect: perception, feeling, will, imaginaton, understanding and reflection. Construed as creative action, knowing is participatory rather than mimetic or representational action. It draws from the sources of life and "pays back" to the common life the "dividend" of an augmented, enlarged, more generous self. Even with all their differences on this the three authors agree: authentic knowledge arises not from acquaintance with life but from participation in the conscious extension of life. The three have in common a certain mysticism, a certain sense of immediacy: the known dwells in the knower, not as something possessed but as something enlivening and intensifying the knower, prompting the pilgrim of reason always still further into the regions of being.

Every literary, philosophical; and theological reputation suffers its fortunes and misfortunes. Edwards, Coleridge, and James have shared in the effects of this law of cyclical renown and eclipse. It is a happy coincidence that today all three are being published again in definitive, critical editions.[6] The immediate future, for them and for us, bodes well.

NOTES

1. *The Notebooks of Samuel Taylor Coleridge*, ed. Kathleen Coburn, 3 volumes to date (Volumes I & II, New York: Pantheon Books, 1957, 1961; Volume III, Princeton: Princeton University Press, 1973), Vol. III, No. 3325.
2. Jonathan Edwards, "The Mind," No. 66, in *The Philosophy of Jonathan Edwards, From His Private Notebooks*, ed. Harvey G. Townsend (Eugene, Oregon: University of Oregon Press, 1955); also in *Scientific and Philosophical Writings*, ed. Wallace E. Anderson, *The Works of Jonathan Edwards*, New Haven: Yale University Press, 1980), Vol. 6.
3. William James, *Pragmatism: A New Name for Some Old Ways of Thinking*, ed. F. Bowers, *The Works of William James*, Vol. 5 (Cambridge, Massachusetts: Harvard University Press, 1975), 138.
4. S. T. Coleridge, *The Literary Remains of Samuel Taylor Coleridge*, ed. H. N. Coleridge, *The Complete Works of S. T. Coleridge*, ed. Shedd (New York: Harper & Brothers, Publishers /1854), Vol. V, 557ff.
5. William James, *A Pluralistic Universe*, ed, F. Bowers, *The Works of William James*, Vol. 4 (Cambridge, Massachusetts: Harvard Untversity Press, 1977), 131.
6. The new edition of Edwards is being published by Yale University Press under the general editorship of John E. Smith. The new Coleridge is being published by Routledge & Kegan Paul and Princeton University Press under the general editorship of Kathleen Coburn. Harvard University Press is publishing *The Works of William James*, with Frederick Burkhardt as general editor.

"LIVING SYMBOLS"
A Chapel Talk

CHANCELLOR Ueno and Professor Ono, colleagues, and friends, I am most grateful to you for the chance to be here as the Neesima lecturer.
I have known Professor Takenaka for many years; I think that it is almost thirty years ago we met. He has suggested to me that today in this chapel talk I be somewhat informal in my remarks and perhaps even a little autobiographical. I have with me a carefully prepared sermon, but I am setting it aside to speak to you more directly and spontaneously.

A little more than a week ago, in the town of Naruko, the manager of the inn in which my colleague and I were staying came to our room and asked: "What is the purpose of your visit?" I could not give him a wholly satisfactory answer on the spur of the moment. But I was able to explain the particular reason for our being in Naruko at that moment. We were trying to follow the path of your great poet Bashō in his journey through the far north. But how to explain my fascination with Bashō and the other reasons for my visit to Japan was something I could not manage on that occasion. Indeed, I cannot even now arrrange the different purposes that have brought me here in an orderly hierarchy. However, I can partially explain the motives of my visit to Japan and to Doshisha University by referring to my life as a teacher.

For the greater part of my adult years I have been a

teacher of theology for students preparing for Christian ministry. More recently, during the last seven years, I have also been a teacher of undergraduates in Harvard College, particularly of young men and women who have chosen to study the great religious traditions of our world. As a teacher of these undergraduates I have worked with my colleagues for some time to find a way of introducing such students to the great religious traditions and also to the religious dimension of human nature. After a good deal of experimentation, we designed an introductory course to the comparative study of religion centering on the topic of pilgrimage, on the different kinds of religious quest that take individuals and bands of people on physical journeys and spiritual adventures through unfamiliar territories. As a result of this work, I have begun to think about our world's religions in new ways.

For example, in biblical history Abraham is not only the paradigm of faith, the one who utterly believed in the promises of God; he is also the incomparable pilgrim of the western world. He obeyed the call of God to leave the home of his fathers and to sojourn in a strange land, which his descendents were to inherit. Similarly, Moses became a pilgrim, albeit unwillingly at first, in response to the summons of God; and he led the children of Israel across the Red Sea and through the wilderness of Sinai to the borders of the promised land. The earliest Christians, as the Letter to the Hebrews describes them, interpreted themselves as enduring in a race, following in a path, blazed by Jesus, the pioneer of their faith, and coming to a heavenly city, the city of the living God. Moreover, for centuries in the past and today on an even greater scale, hundreds of thousads of Muslims each year re-enact the wanderings of Hagar and Ishmael and the return of the prophet, Mohammed, to Mecca in the great pilgrimage called the Hajj. And in these times in the United States, as the meaning of the history of our origins grows in importance to us, Americans increasingly look back to the generation of Governor Bradford and John Winthrop and their companions who crossed the "Red Sea" of the Atlantic Ocean, thinking of themselves as re-enacting Israel's journey to Canaan to establish a new "city on a hill" in the wilderness of New England.

And here in Japan in the last ten days or so, I have encountered many pilgrims, at Nikko and Hiraizumi and elsewhere, visting various shrines and temples and monuments.

One kind of pilgrimage takes the sojourner through a passage toward a geographically definable goal. Most of the pilgrimages I have mentioned are of that kind, even though the events that transpire along the way may become as important as the action of reaching the goal. There is another kind of pilgrimage, the goal of which is to discover or to recover one's true self or one's true home. Pilgrimage of this sort may involve a journey or it may involve an abiding in one place. But the purpose of travelling or of dwelling is to penetrate ordinary experience and to discern the brilliance that is hidden within its ordinariness. In my country Henry David Thoreau (1817-1862) is one well known example of a pilgrim with this purpose; he travelled but a few miles to settle down in his beloved Walden woods. And here in Japan Bashō (1644-1694), who travels repeatedly, who makes pilgrimage casting away his possessions and finally casting away

himself in order to discover his everlasting self, is another great example. I would like to read, in translation, a portion of what Bashō wrote having to do with his purposes. He says:
> What is important is to keep our mind high in the world of true understanding, and returning to the world of our daily experience to seek therein the truth of beauty.

Then he goes on as follows:
> No matter what we may be doing at a given moment, we must not forget that it has a bearing upon our everlasting self which is poetry.*

Ever since reading these words a number of years ago, I have been captivated by this poet-traveller, even though I cannot appreciate his full subtlety in his own language.

I should like to explain why it is that he has captivated me. Bashō presents a truth of life, of all experience, which I formulate for myself in this way: We must each of us learn how to become generous. I use the word *generous* because it is allied to and draws part of its meaning from the words *genus*, *kin* and *kindred*, and *kind*. So to become generous is to become open to all one's kin, to all the members of one's kind, thus to all the members of the human race and—ultimately—to the very earth itself, which is the larger body we share. Therefore, our task, my task, is so to orient myself in my travelling and in my abiding in one place that the neighbour and the human family and the natural environment may enter into myself.

Poets are makers, and in making poems they make themselves. Now Bashō is a poet of genius. Not all of us are poets of genius. But we are all poets in this sense: we

---
* *The Narrow Road to the Deep North and Other Travel Sketches*; trans. & ed. Nobuyuki Yuasa (New York: Penguin Books, 1977), p. 28.

make ourselves, we create ourselves, by the attitudes and responses we cultivate toward the social and natural worlds surrounding us. If we do not attend to our responsibilities as poets, in this larger sense that I have mentioned, if we do not try to shape ourselves and our responses to our world so that we become more open, then we remain shut up in the privacy and prison of our individual selfhood. So to become open or generous requires of us that we practice our poetic abilities. To become generous places a heavy demand on our imagination.

I have come to believe over the last ten or fifteen years that we dwell in our world according to the way in which we imagine our world. And the way in which we imagine the world depends upon the images we deliberately or unconsciously choose. If we do not deliberately choose images on which to meditate, then images will choose us and become the laws of our thinking. We cannot pierce through our old habits to the real world except as we imagine this world as faithfully, as critically, and as responsibly as lies in our power.

Each of us is like a mother who carries the world as a child. The world lives in us according to the purity and fidelity of our imagination. By carrying the world in ourselves and in our imaginations we become symbols, living symbols of our world. And if we imagine faithfully and critically, then the world comes to new life in ourselves; and we in turn give something of ourselves to the world.

I believe the great responsibility we all have on this green earth is the responsibility of seeing, which is the same as the responsibility of imagining. Let me refer to the Scripture lesson that was read in the service this morning. In the King James Version of the New Testament, Matthew 6:22 reads: "If therefore thine eye be single, thy whole body shall be full of light." The Japanese translation used this morning is, I think, more direct, because it reads "If your eye is clear. . . ." But the reason, I believe, that the King James Version says "If therefore thine eye be single" is as follows. Our eyes and all our senses are like pieces of paper which have been folded over many times. This is the result of our habits. Our habits, which should be only temporary dwellings, like the tents of nomads, we allow to become the permanent houses in which we are shut up. Our habits become our habitations. To make our vision clear means to unwrap the habits of our imaginations that enfold our minds and hearts and keep out the light and the world.

Ultimately, seeing and imagining depend on purity of heart. Seeing and imagining in order to become generous and open rather than prisoners of the familiar is a religious task. Therefore, I believe, this verse in the Gospel according to Matthew applies to all poets and hence to all of us. If your eye is single, that is not folded, then your whole body shall be full of light, that is full of the amazing life that surrounds us. I believe the journey of imagination, in which we pierce through the ordinary, is one for which we are all accountable. I have long wished to visit Japan in order to make a significant part of this journey for myself. I am grateful to you for making the journey possible.

(Delivered at Divinity Hall Chapel, Doshisha University, 7 May 1980)

First Lecture

"BEING IS PROPORTION" JONATHAN EDWARDS' PHILOSOPHY OF EXCELLENCY

Introduction

JONATHAN Edwards belongs to a company of men and women whose intellect and religious faith so energize each other that they are able to range into spiritual and metaphysical regions where few others venture and to return with charts of the amplitude of being which enlarge our horizons. Faith, in these persons, is less an independent action of will or of some other special faculty of mind or soul than it is the life and the spirit of the whole intelligence. Faith is the vessel that carries the mind from its first glimpse of wonder to the far country where its eye is opened wide and drenched by visions of glory. These men and women are mystic travelers exploring the infinite. Yet in another sense they are not travelers at all but rather contemplatives, minutely inspecting the cirumstances of their daily lives. They interrogate the world disclosed to them in their own experience, seeking there the patterns and signatures of divinity, what Edwards called "the proportion of God's acting."[1]

1. Edwards' "Empiricism"

Jonathan Edwards, born in 1703, spent his childhood in the Connecticut River Valley in the town of East

Windsor, about forty miles north of New Haven, where Yale College permanently settled itself during Edwards' student days. In this broad valley Edwards began to awaken to the excitement and to the pleasure which the observation of nature offers, and at some point while he was still a youth he started recording his observations, together with the questions they prompted and the solutions he proposed.[2] The best known of these early written observations is an account Edwards made of the behavior of certain spiders and other "flying " insects that he had apparently long noticed in the meadows and thickets around his father's parsonage. The title this account bears is "Of Insects." It displays a number of the traits distinctive of his later treatises and sermons, traits for which Edwards is now well known in the history of American letters: vivacity, exactitude in description, and a simple cadence of considerable charm. The essay "Of Insects" revolves around the question, how these spiders "march in the air," as its author puts it, or move from bush to bush and tree to tree without descending to the ground.[3]

> [I] know I have several times seen in a very Calm and serene Day at that time of the year, standing behind some Opake body that shall Just hide the Disk of the sun and keep of his Dazling rays from my eye and looking close by the side of it, multitudes of little shining webbs and Glistening Strings of a Great length and at such a height as that one would think they were tack'd to the Sky by the one end were it not that they were moving and floating, and there Very Often appears at the end of the Webs a Spider floating and sailing in

the air with them, which I have Plainly Discerned in those webs that were nearer to my eye and Once saw a very large spider to my surprise swimming in the air in this manner . . . the appearance is truly very Pretty And Pleasing and it was so pleasing as well as surprising to me that I Resolved to endeavour to Satisfy my Curiosity about it by findng Out the way and manner of their Doing it, being also Persuaded that If I could find out how they flew I could also easily find out how they made webs from tree to tree . . .

The reader familiar with Edwards can recognize in this early example of his writing several characteristic features, not the least of these being the author's evident determination to decipher this riddle. But there are other qualities present as well, of which the following are especially relevant to Edwards' philosophy of excellency: (1) the author's visual quickness, a symptom of his perceptual alertness in general; (2) the corresponding directness and spiritedness of his language; (3) and the sheer pleasure he takes in the sight of these creatures "swimming in the air." This last mentioned element in the composition, its emphasis upon the pleasingness of the appearance of the sailing spiders, takes on added meaning as we become mindful of the fact that in his early and later philosophical reflections Edwards frequently returns to the theme of the pleasure attending "a new perception," especially a perception that discovers beings in harmonious, proportional relation to other beings. Indeed, when Edwards reaches the point of describing the end or purpose for which God created the world, he names that end as the happiness of intelligent beings; and the "nature" of their happiness, he explains, lies in the perception of the consent of being to being, in "the perception of excellency."[4]

The essay on the spiders shows one of the important attributes of the genuinely empirical mind: thirst for knowledge by direct acquaintance, for knowledge mediated by sense and not by conventionalized signs or words alone.

When it was that Edwards first read John Locke's *Essay Concerning Human Understanding* is a matter about which historians make conjectures without being able to reach certitude. Whether it was before or after his initial "essay" on the spiders or between the "essay" and the writing of a subsequent letter on the subject remains unsettled. In time, Edwards came to use Locke's distinction between "simple ideas," ideas that are furnished to the mind by sense perception or by reflection on sense perception, and "complex ideas," ideas that are fabricated by the mind out of its simple ideas. The idea of substance is a principal example of such mental compounds. Edwards' language also echoes another of Locke's distinctions, roughly parallel to the first; it is the distinction between words used as names of simple ideas or of elementary mental compounds of simple ideas and words used as names of mental abstractions, such as words naming a class or species or genus. We customarily employ words of this latter sort without having in mind the way in which these words originated in sense or in reflection on sense. Hence, while we do not know when Edwards first seriously meditated on Locke's revolutionary essay, it is evident to us that Edwards adopted themes of Locke's philosophy as instruments of his own thinking.

Yet Edwards never was a Lockean or even an empiricist in the ordinary, rather imprecise and restrictive senses of those words, which suggest that the mind is passive in its getting of knowledge, that the mind is not only metaphorically but unambiguously a "white tablet" or blank, empty sheet. To be sure, Edwards valued knowledge by direct acquaintance more than any other kind. But he judged the mind to be active as well, to be animated by will and disposition. Intellectual or rational will and desire make the difference between the minds of beasts and the human mind. This conviction is fundamental to Edwards' empiricism.

In order to appreciate the larger meaning of Edwards' empiricism, one must take into account the evident disposition of his own mind toward admiration, toward what he called "the passion of admiration," an intellectual appetite that enabled him to derive such pleasure from, among other things, the world of nature. Moreover, the strength of this passion owed a good deal to Edwards' religious nurture, for he, like other citizens of the 18th century and like other Puritans, responded not only to the example of Isaac Newton and to the adventure of first-hand inquiry and observation but also to the example of David the singer, to the language and music of the Bible and especially of the Psalms. Indeed, Edwards lived in the Psalms and thus in some of the most vibrant poetry of nature that Christendom has known. His preaching and his brief autobiographical account of his conversion experiences as a young man make this plain. In his "Personal Narrative," written sometime after 1739, Edwards tells us that then he walked alone in his father's pasture and contemplated in the sky and the earth the glorious majesty of God, and that on these solitary walks he conversed with Christ and sang forth his own thoughts with a "sweet burning in his heart." As the Psalmist exclaimed: "O Lord, our Lord, how majestic is thy name in all the earth!" so Edwards chanted the glory of God in his river valley.[5]

> The appearance of everything was altered; there seemed to be, as it were, a calm sweet cast, or appearance of divine glory, in almost everything. God's excellency, his wisdom, his purity and love, seemed to appear in every thing; in the sun, moon, and stars; in the clouds, and blue sky; in the grass, flowers, trees; in the water, and all nature; which used greatly to fix my mind. I often used to sit and view the moon for continuance; and in the day, spent much time in viewing the clouds and sky, to behold the sweet glory of God in these things; in the mean time, singing forth, with a low voice my contemplations of the Creator and Redeemer.

Members of an earlier generation spoke of their souls as being well or ill turned to magnify God, thereby testifying to the lasting appeal of music as an analogy for the nature of the soul. Jonathan Edwards' perceptual responsiveness to the world or book of nature owes much to the fact that the songs of David tuned his soul.

Even today commentators who should be well informed occasionally fail to take note of the great variety of temperaments among the people we call Puritans. Hence we still need to remind ourselves not to overlook the mysticism and lyricism to which the Puritan soul rises in generation after generation. For the Puritans are as susceptible to ecstasy as any religious person. Moreover, from them, along with the Quakers, we have a series of spiritual testimonies that makes a distinctive chapter in western literature. The best known of these spiritual autobiographies is John Bunyan's *Grace Abounding To The Chief of Sinners*. Next to Bunyan's book Edwards' "Personal Narrative" appears as but a small link in that series. Nevertheless, it arrests our attention because it not only tells about the author's religious experience but it does so in a vocabulary and system of ideas that Edwards had carefully developed over a period of years. Consequently we learn from the "Personal Narrative" both a good deal about the qualities of Edwards' "conversion" and mystic communion with God and a good deal about the way in which Edwards approached the description and interpretation of religious experience. What the "Personal Narrative" signifies, among other things, is that Edwards could and did turn his attention with equal force of concentration from objects in nature to moments in spiritual experience. He had the same intense, involved interest in mystical rapture that he had in spiders. This characteristic is all the more apparent from the fact that Edwards scrutinized the religious experience and testimonies of others as well, and the "Personal Narrative" is only one of a number of compositions concerning religious awakening written during the 1730's and 1740's. In fact, the body of literature Edwards left behind shows him to be one of the most skilled interpreters of religious experience to have appeared in the modern west. On the North American continent he probably has no peer.

2. "Excellency"

In the "Personal Narrative" Edwards wrote:"... my mind was greatly engaged to spend my time in reading and meditating on Christ, on the beauty and excellency of his person, and the lovely way of salvation by free grace in him."[6] Again, later in the narrative he recalled: [7]

> Once, as I rode out into the woods for my health, in 1737, having alighted from my horse in a retired place ... to walk for divine contemplation and prayer .... The person of Christ appeared ineffably excellent with an excellency great enough to swallow up all thought and conception.... which continued as near as I can judge, about an hour.

Throughout his life Edwards used this word excellency to characterize Christ, to characterize God both as the first person and as the unity of the three persons of the Trinity; and he spoke of the Holy Spirit in language of a similar tendency, describing it as "an infinite fountain of divine glory and sweetness ... pouring forth itself in sweet communications; like the sun in its glory, sweetly and pleasantly diffusing light and life."[8] However, the word excellency not only repeats itself with great frequency in Edwards' discourse; it bears a special range of meanings which are central to his account of his own religious experience and equally to his reasoning about religion more generally and about God.

We can follow Edwards' thinking about such experience and about God by taking note of the elements of meaning which the term excellency conveys. To do this we turn to an important series of notes entitled "The

Mind," which Edwards began, apparently, about a year after leaving Yale. (1) First of all, in its most restricted sense, excellency refers to that kind of natural beauty which Edwards called "simple beauty." It appears in any plain, simple geometrical figure, such as a square or rectangle or equilateral triangle. Each of these figures is a system of equal relations, that is, of relations which directly correspond with each other, which are *equal* to each other, and so *agree* with each other. The perpendicular sides of the rectangle are in simple agreement, and so are all the sides and angles of the equilateral triangle. These are instances of "simple beauty," which may be found in abundance in objects in nature, for example, in spiders' webs and in the patterns that the branches of the young tree make with their trunk. Edwards' notes on nature contain many observations of phenomena showing these simple equalities, the most elementary kind of regularity, in which there is simple agreement of angle with angle, line with line, and force with force.[9]

(2) But we take a significant step forward into the larger meaning of the term excellency, when we advance with Edwards from "simple" to "complex beauty." In doing so, we shift our attention from relation involving equality only to relations involving proportionality as well. In an object showing proportional beauty, the "agreement" or "agreeableness" — to use Edwards' terms — lies not between lines or angles of identical magnitude but between lines or figures of different magnitudes which nevertheless "fit" together in what we call a harmonious way. And that, indeed, is the root meaning of the English word harmony: a fitting or joining of

parts in such a fashion that the result is pleasing. In the chrysanthemum the concentric circles of petals are proportionally or harmoniously agreeable to each other. In the chambered nautilus the segments of the shell joined together in an expanding spiral are ever larger, as we follow the spiral from its center to its terminus on the periphery, yet these segments of different sizes are proportionally related and agreeable to each other. Nature shows us millions of this kind of complex beauty, Edwards said.

> That sort of beauty which is called natural, as of vines, plants, etc., consists of a very complicated harmony.[10]

To complex beauty that appears pre-eminently in fixed visual patterns, Edwards added the complex beauty that arises from proportionally related motions. The motions of bodies in earth's space, of the planets, the moon, the sun, and the stars, come immediately to mind in this connection, but there is also the dynamic phenomenon of "flow," the current of air, for example, that sets fallen leaves astir in an eddy or the shallow stream of water that carries the bubbles on its surface all in one direction. And then Edwards further observed that proportional motion is involved in all the pleasures of the senses, for example, in the vibrations of the air that strike the ear. "And so, in the pleasantness of light, colors, tastes, smells, and touch—all arise from proportion of motion."[11] Edwards mentions the beauty of the human body and face more than once in his reflections on excellency in "The Mind." There appears to be several reasons he does so. One paragraph suggests it is because our bodies and faces, like other natural forms, contain many irregularities and disproportions, which, however, enhance their complex beauty as wholes. For, as Edwards wrote, particular disproportions can contribute to a larger, more comprehensive beauty. In such configurations we discern a more intense beauty, a beauty that aproaches "a more universal proportion."[12]

(3) Here we are at a third important step in Edwards' initial analysis of excellency. It is the discrimination he makes of that feature in complex beauty which renders it of lesser or greater intensity, the feature which moves it nearer to or further away from the ideal of "universal proportion." The example to which Edwards alludes, the human face and body, helps us to understand him. For we observe that the human form is proportionally related to many of the other figures and patterns the natural world offers to us. Painting, sculpture and photography show this proportional relation in an almost infinite variety of ways. Within a face or a bodily form there are always particular irregularities. However, what appear to be disproportions when we consider a bodily form simply for itself, turn out to be elements which, when we consider it in the fabric of its larger environment, relate the form beautifully to other objects in the environment. The human figure approaches to proportional universality because it "agrees" with so many other natural figures and forms. And it could not "agree" with so many other figures and forms, if it did not have within itself some inequalities and disproportions.

Now we have one of the most important judgments that Edwards made, one that is central to his natural philosophy or reflection on being and equally central to his theological philosophy or reflection on spiritual being.

The capacity of a body of complex beauty to display proportional relations within an ever enlarging sphere means that the body is beautiful not only in itself but —what is of more importance—is beautiful in relation to others. And the more intensely beautiful an object is, the greater is its capacity to join in affirmative relations to the most diverse kinds of other beings. Such an object may "agree" to the stars, to the trees, to rocks, and to ocean waves. Again, if we consider the human form, we note that it does relate proportionally to all of these other bodies. Poets and painters have portrayed these proportional relations throughout history. We come to the conclusion, then, that intense natural beauty mediates between objects that are apparently disparate. It conjoins them. It reconciles them. Furthermore, we note that the means by which it reconciles or conjoins these diverse objects is by being "agreeable" to them, that is, by being proportionally related to them.

The very nature, Edwards went on to say, the very being of a beautiful thing is its proportionality. Therefore, what a beautiful object is in itself, that is, proportion, is also the object's relation to other beings. Edwards summarizes all these steps in his fundamental analysis of excellency in the following general thesis:

> For being, if we examine narrowly, is nothing else but proportion.[13]

Edwards does not use the word ontology. It is not a part of his vocabulary. However, if we employ it, we should say that the foundation of his ontology, the foundation of his philosophy of being, lies in proportionality or in complex, intense beauty. In fact, Edwards' ethics is founded on this conviction as well. Where being agrees with being there is more entity. Where being is disagreeable to being there is "an approach to nothing, or a degree of nothing."[14]

We have followed Edwards' reflections as a young man through the first stages of his philosophy of excellency, that with which we are more concerned, he believed, than with anything else. (1) Excellency is beauty, and the first kind of beauty we recognize is the beauty of simple equality. (2) But proportion gives us a higher, more complex beauty, a more universal beauty. (3) A figure or body made up of proportions that include particular disproportions has greater intensity and has the capacity to be related, to be "agreeable," to other different and diverse entities. This progression issues in the first general thesis of Edwards' philosophy of excellency: *being is proportion*. The converse of this thesis is that "disagreeableness" to other entity is the contradiction of being. It is "an approach to nothing." The word excellency, therefore, stands for the very nature of being. It is for all of these reasons that Edwards declared: "One alone without any reference to any more cannot be excellent."[15] The immediate inference is that indivisible unity, a unity which admits of no proportionality, utter simplicity, is the absence of being.

3. Nature as God's Language

In these earliest sustained reflections on excellency Edwards hastened on to say that bodies showing us such complex beauty are "shadows of being," that is, shadows of a more intense and comprehensive kind of being, and their proportions are correspondingly "shadows" of more universal proportions. What he had in mind is that nature foreshadows spirit and that natural beauty foreshadows spiritual beauty. Consequently, Edwards reasoned, nature rightly discerned presents us with a grammar of spirit, a language of God.

New Englanders of a later generation adopted this principle with enthusiasm. Ralph Waldo Emerson constructed his first full book upon it. Emerson, to be sure, drew from other sources as well, among them Thomas Carlyle and Samuel Taylor Coleridge. Moreover, he rejected the institutional religion of New England in which Edwards had played so important a part. Nevertheless, Edwards' great themes as well as those of Puritanism in general echoed clearly in Emerson's rhetoric. "Nature," he declared, "is the symbol of spirit."[16] And subsequently he added that nature "is an inferior incarnation of God"; it is "the present expositor of the divine mind."[17] So intimate is the connection which nature provides between human beings and the divine, Emerson exclaimed, that when we worthily participate in nature we also participate in the life of deity itself.[18]

In the woods we return to reason and faith. . . .
Standing on the bare ground—my head bathed by the blithe air and uplifted into infinite space—all mean egoism vanishes. I become a transparent eyeball; I am nothing; I see all; the currents of Universal Being circulate through me; I am part or parcel of God.

Henry David Thoreau wrote to the same effect though in a less didactic and more poetic manner. According to Thoreau, nature provides us with "a sweet and beneficent society." "*Next* to us is not the workman whom we have hired, with whom we love so well to talk, but the workman whose work we are."[19] In the minds of Emerson and Thoreau nature is a means, indeed it is *the* means, of refreshing the innocence of childhood. As Emerson put the matter: "The lover of nature is he whose inward and outward senses are still truly adjusted to each other; who has retained the spirit of infancy into the era of manhood."[20]

Emerson and Thoreau share the conviction that each of us is a divine being "in ruins," and nature can restore us, regenerate us, return us to the morning of creation. This religion of divine nature pervaded American culture in the 19th century. Its influence is to be seen in literature and in painting, in folklore and in politics—and not only in the 19th century but in the 20th as well, particularly in the new religion of nature today, which is so closely intertwined with ecology and the general concern to preseve the natural wildness of the earth. The presence of this religious sensibility is especially clear in the landscape art of some of our most distinguised photographers.[21]

Jonathan Edwards is not the sole source of this grand theme in American cultural history, but he is one of its clearest sources. According to him also, God communicates with us through nature. Indeed, Edwards said, the world is to God as the body is to the mind.[22] Therefore, to perceive nature rightly is to perceive the wisdom of God, the moral government of God, the signs and emblems of God's providential ways with human kind. Edwards regarded nature as a great treasury of images and shadows of divine truths. He noted that Christ often made use of things that belong to the very constitution of the world, such as the harvest, the birds of the air, foxes, the mountains, as evidence of the truth of what he said.[23] And Edwards meditated on the spiritual and divine meaning of rivers, of mountains and hills, of thunder and thunder clouds, of the waves and billows of the sea, of the sun and moon and stars, of lightning, and of many other particular phenomena of nature.

4. Consent and Agreement

However, Edwards developed his conviction that nature is a system of images and shadows of divine things —a system of symbols—through his close reflections on the action of perceiving natural beauty and, more generally, on the action of perceiving excellency, whether in nature or in society. It is here that we can see his thinking following a course different from the course Emerson, Thoreau and other later Americans followed. Edwards' idea of perception makes all the difference, for he believed, not that nature restores us, but rather that the gracious, living fountain of nature restores us by freshening and deepening and expanding our perceiving. Consequently, we need to return to Edwards' first general thesis about excellency that being is nothing else but proportion, and take up the logic of the further development of his idea of excellency, which will lead us to one of the crowning themes of his philosophy, theology, and preaching: the theme of the "new spiritual sense" by which the saints enjoy an "entirely new kind of perception" or "spiritual sense."[24]

We have already attended to Edwards' saying, "One alone without reference to any more cannot be excellent." The reason "one alone" cannot be excellent is that "one alone" cannot exist in proportional relation to anything. Furthermore, we have gathered that Edwards held proportion to be an expansive, dynamic relation. That, at least, is the direct inference from the fact that it is complex and not simple beauty which can approach to a universal proportion. It is evident that as Edwards used the word proportion, it is the name of an action. "The lowest or most simple kind of beauty," he wrote in "The Mind," "is equality or likeness, because by equality or likeness one part consents with but one part. But by proportion one part may sweetly consent to ten thousand different parts."[25]

Edwards customarily employed two verbs to express this activity of two or more things existing together or coming together in an expansive relation. These are the verbs "agree" and "consent." They work on at least three levels of meaning in his philosophy of excellency. (1) They may signify the *similarity* of two or more forms, as they do were we to say that the shape of the sand dune and the shape of the ocean wave "agree" with one another or "consent" to each other. Of course, today speakers of English are not likely to put their thoughts in just this manner. But our linguistic usage is sufficiently close to that of the 18th century that we understand what such a locution means. In any case, agreement or consent involving no more than an easily or casually noticed resemblance signifies relation of a low order, a low intensity. (2) They may signify the enjoyment of pleasure or even happiness (in the strict, classical sense of that term: well being), as they do when we say that the sight of the autumn leaves "agrees" with us more than does the sight of spring blossoms; or that the harvest moon "consents," that is, "harmonizes," more with our mood than does the winter sun. On this second level the agreement' or "consent" are more complex than on the first level, because more of the activity of the whole mind of the perceiver is explicitly involved, for example, the perceiver's disposition as well as capacity to judge resemblances. (3) They may signify an action of willing, as they do if we affirm that we "agree" with or "consent" to Jesus' maxim that where our treasure is there will our hearts be also. Each of these levels or spheres of meaning is important; and all of them may be at work at the same time. But the second is more complex than the first, and the third more complex than the second, because "agreement" or "consent" progressively symbolizes a denser state of affairs, a richer interaction between perceiver and perceived. As we ascend from one level to the next we meet with a mounting intensity of relation or being. Therefore, Edwards cautioned, the "proper" meaning of "consent" appears when we speak of "spiritual things," by which he meant the "consent" that involves perceiving and willing at their maximum, in other words, the "consent" that is love. "When we spake of excellence in bodies, we were obliged to borrow the word 'consent' from spiritual things."[26] "This is an universal definition of excellency," Edwards wrote: "The consent of being to being, or being's consent to entity. The more the consent is, and the more extensive, the greater is the excellency."[27]

In order more fully to understand how the intensity of relation or being mounts as we move from the lower to the highest level of agreement and consent, we need to pay closer attention to the ways in which these spheres of meaning interpenetrate each other. To achieve this purpose, we will meditate with Edwards while having before us an example of proportion or excellemcy drawn from nature, an example as familiar to Edwards as to ourselves: the spider's web. And we will proceed by marking as we go each step of Edwards' thinking.

Step 1 - The web between the two stems of wild grass makes a figured "object" in nature, exhibiting many simple equalities between line and line, angle and angle. But simple agreement does not entirely prevail, for there are many irregularities and inequalities. The web and grass together exhibit complex beauty or proportion. Therefore, the "object" as a whole shows us excellency. Edwards defined excellency as the "consent of being to being." Here, though this figured object is but a shadow of "spiritual things," each part of the object "sweetly consents" to hundreds of other parts.

Step 2 - When we consider the figured object as an object the mind *perceives*, we shift our attention to the mind's idea of this bodily proportion or excellence. Edwards called an idea directly deriving from perception an "actual idea." "Actual ideas" differ from ideas aroused indirectly, ideas which arise in the mind through association with a word or other sign but are not fresh impressions of the things signified.[28] Moreover, an "actual idea" is a "repetition" in the mind of the thing perceived.[29] Hence, through our perceiving it, the web-between-the-stalks-of-grass exists "over again" in our minds; it exists a second time as "actual idea" of an excellency.

Step 3 - As we further meditate on this natual proportion existing in the mind as "actual idea," we become more sharply aware of the figure's agreeableness to us. We observe that the proportion, the consent of being to being within the figure as a whole, gives us *pleasure*. But the experience of pleasure suggests that more is at work in perceiving and in having an "actual idea" than sense perception alone. The mind's "inclination to perceive the things that are," the "passion of admiration," the mind's "desire"—all these are active in perceiving and in enjoying an "actual idea" of an excellency.

Step 4 - Through reflection on these first three steps we become aware that the mind is entering into a "conversation" with its "actual idea" of excellency and is experiencing a measure of delight.[30] We become aware that the mind is more than a simple unity. In its "appetite" for such "actual ideas" the mind manifests itself as active, alive, and twofold. It is perceiving, understanding mind *and* desiring, willing mind, experiencing agreement between its "actual idea" of the figured object and its inclination and desire. The nature of mind is energy or dynamism. The mind is dynamic relation.

Step 5 - We have become conscious that the agreement between the parts of the complex figure of web and wild grass echoes in the mind. The excellency of the figure is repeated in the mind as pleasure. But this pleasure is more than an echo of the figure's beauty. It is a coming alive a second time of that proportionality. It is an extension, an enlargement, and therefore an intensification of the proportion appearing in the figure. We see, then, that there is consent, an augmenting relation, between mind and the excellent nature of the object.

Step 6 - As the mind reflects more on its "actual idea" of this natural beauty, it prolongs its internal conversation. In this manner, the mind expands, as it were, and the twofoldness and dynamism of the mind becomes more apparent. The nature of mind as *consciousness* grows more evident. Edwards, in fact, compares the mind to a society whose members are rejoicing in their conversation about an excellent, "actual idea." The mind in conversation with itself about its idea of an excellency is an image of the divine society of the Godhead.

Step 7 - Edwards described this quality or intensification of consciousness as "happiness." "Happiness," Edwards wrote, " . . . is the perception of excellency."[31] And we may convert this statement into its mirror image: excellency perceived by and come alive in consciousness is happiness.

Step 8 - Deeper meditation reveals that this happiness cannot be accidental. On the contrary, it is the very fulfillment of our own being. As Edwards put the matter, the purpose or end for which God created the world is for intelligent beings to be "the consciousness of the world" and to be happy in "the perception of excellency."[32]

We have now taken eight measured steps with Edwards in his philosophy of excellency. Of course, we might have made the number five or fifteen. What matters is that we have tried to enter with Edwards into the process of his thinking. But it may be helpful to pause on this path along which we have come and to survey the view as a whole that it offers us. When we take the figured natural beauty, the web and the stems of grass, and join it with the perceiving, conscious, happy mind, which repeats the bodily excellency and delights in it, then we can recognize that the minds' acts of perceiving and thinking the natural excellency create an increment, an enlargement of excellency, of proportion, and hence of being. To "have" an "actual idea" of beauty or proportion in the only way in which mind can "have" anything is to be active about the idea. To have the "actual idea" of proportion in a lively way and to be happy in consenting to it is to add beauty to beauty, proportion to proportion, and being to being. We can then understand why Edwards so ardently believed that the duty of the saint is to behold the beauty of the things that are. Edwards' mystical empiricism or empirical mysticism expresses the vocation of human beings to add to the excellency of the created world.

Only a mind that is fully alive, however, can carry out this vocation. Such a mind beholds the parts of an excellency in nature, such as the spider's web, the grass, the trees, the clouds, the thunder, as though they are members of "a society of many perceiving beings sweetly agreeing to each other."[33] The true beauty of nature expresses the divine mind. The proportions of nature show to the saint "the proportions of God's acting."[34] Nature's excellency repeated in the mind is the shadowing or mirroring of divine glory.

5. The New Spiritual Sense

When as a young man Edwards walked alone in the pastures near his father's house in the Connecticut River valley and perceived the excellency of God and of Christ in all that met his eyes and ears, while singing forth the words of the Psalms and his own meditations, he was sharing in the rejoicing of the Creator, a rejoicing that throbs throughout all creation. This rejoicing is the great chorus of being: the universal consent of being to being. Experience had taught Edwards that the hindrance which ever besets us mortals is that we are restricted in our affections, in our consent to being, in our love, and hence in our knowledge. We content ourselves with verbal significations of things that are no more than verbal, with speaking about things by arbitrary signs and conventional names without waiting to know them in the fullness of their actuality. But experience had equally taught Edwards that the highest degree of human participation in excellency is realized when we become willing partners in the divine perception of the world and, correspondingly, when we become aware of this perception of the world as a "new spiritual sensation."[35] True knowledge, which is the knowledge that transforms the knower, takes place in us as our senses—our vision, our taste, our hearing, our touch—are enlivened by a new spiritual sense, which is the gift of the presence in us of the Holy Spirit.

As we noticed when we listened to Edwards' account of the spiders in the meadows, he was especially alert to the ways in which the rays of light strike the spiders' webs, causing them to glisten and so to stir wonder in the mind. The ordinarily invisible webs become refractors and prisms of the light falling upon them. Something analogous happens in the life of the saint whose capacities for perception are vivified by the Spirit of God. (Indeed, such vivification is one of the principal marks of what Edwards understood saintliness to be.) The perceiving mind of the saint no longer merely *works* as a passive instrument registering the reflected rays of the sun; instead it *acts* as a living organ of direct spiritual vision, transmitting and emitting spiritual light. The saint, apprehending directly in this fashion, is a "lightsome body," a new source of light, adding to the brilliance of the totality of what is.[36]

The foregoing pages have sketched only the foundations of Jonathan Edwards' philosophy of excellency. The richness of his developed thinking about perception, consent, and complex beauty is without rival on the North American continent. It constitutes a marriage of empiricism and mysticism not to be found elsewhere. Two treatises of his, published posthumously, *The End for Which God Created the World* and *The Nature of True Virture* exhibit the fruition of these principles; but the exploration of these two treatises lies outside the limits of our present brief engagement with Edwards' idea of excellency. Nevertheless, it may be fitting to close with a simple indication of the direction in which Edwards' religious thinking and vision ultimately extended: To apprehend with the energy of spiritual consent to or love of that which is excellent is to take part in the enlargement of being in general and so in the enlargement of the divie life itself.

NOTES

1. The phrase "the proportion of God's acting" occurs in Entry No. 34 of "The Mind." The most accessible edited texts of "The Mind" are in *The Philosophy of Janathan Edwards, From His Private Notebooks*, ed. Harvey G. Townsend (Eugene, Oregon: University of Oregon Press, 1955), hereafter cited as *HGT*; and in *Scientific and Philosophical Writings*, ed. Wallace E. Anderson (New Haven: Yale University Press, 1980), hereafter cited as *WEA*. The latter is volume six of the currently appearing Yale University Press edition of *The Works of Janathan Edwards*. In the following notes citations of and references to "The Mind" include page numbers for both *HGT* and *WEA*. For the phrase quoted, see *HGT*, p.39 and *WEA*, p. 353.
2. Anderson recounts the history of editorial opinion about the dates of composition of the essay "Of Insects" and "Of the Rainbow" as well as of the series of entries bearing the title "The Mind." Drawing on the research of Thomas Schafer, Anderson places the essays somewhat later than did earlier prevailing conjecture, i.e. during Edwards' student years at Yale. Whatever the precise date, "Of Insects," like "Of the Rainbow," refers to Edwards' observation of natural phenomena in the neighborhood of his childhood home. Anderson believes that Edwards began "The Mind" in 1723, approximately a year after he concluded his graduate studies at Yale. If so, Edwards was twenty years old when he started his all important sustained inquiry into excellency.
3. *WEA*, p. 154f. Anderson has considerably modernized Edwards' text, to the point of obliterating stylistic characteristics. I have therefore quoted from an earlier publication of the text. See Egbert C. Smyth, "The Flying Spider—Observations by Jonathan Edwards When A Boy; from an unpublished manuscript," *The Andover Review*, Vol. XIII, No. LXXIII, Jan. 1890; p. 8.
4. *Miscellanies*, No. 87, *HGT*, p. 128f. A complete text of Edwards' miscellaneous observations, on philosophical and theological matters, on Scripture, etc., is still to be published. Townsend

has included a selection of them in the work cited, among them the important entry, No. 782 "Ideas, Sense of the heart." Concerning the central role of pleasure in perception, see "The Mind," Entry No. 1 throughout, *HGT*, pp. 21ff. & *WEA*, pp. 332ff. and also Entry No. 49. The posthumously published treatise, *Dissertation Concerning The End For Which God Created The World*, places the rejoicing of the saint within the rejoicing of the Godhead in its own glory.

5. The "Personal Narrative" is accessible in several anthologies of Edwards' writings. The most useful is *Jonathan Edwards: Representative Selections, With Introduction, Bibliography & Notes*, ed. C. H. Faust & T. H. Johnson, revised edition (New York: Hill & Wang, 1962). The sentences quoted are on p. 60f.
6. *Edwards: Representative Selections*, p. 59f.
7. *Edwards: Representative Selections*, p. 69.
8. *Edwards: Representative Selections*, p. 69.
9. See "Things to be Considered & Written fully about," No. 48, for example, in *WEA*, pp. 242ff.
10. "The Mind," No. 1, *HGT*, p. 24; *WEA*, p. 335.
11. "The Mind," No. 1, *HGT*, p. 24; *WEA*, p. 336.
12. "The Mind," No. 1, *HGT*, p. 24; *WEA*, p. 335.
13. "The Mind," No. 1. *HGT*, p. 25; *WEA*, p. 336.
14. "The Mind." No. 1, *HGT*, p. 24; *WEA*, p. 335.
15. "The Mind," No. 1, *HGT*, p. 26; *WEA*, p. 337.
16. Chapter IV, "Language," *Nature*; in *Selected Essays, Lectures, and Poems of Ralph Waldo Emerson*, ed. R. E. Spiller (New York: Washington Square Press, 1965), p. 190.
17. Emerson, *Selected Essays*, p. 211f.
18. Emerson,*Selected Essays*, p. 182.
19. H. D. Thoreau, *Walden*, ed. J. L. Shanley (Princeton: Princeton Universty Press, 1971), p. 134.
20. Emerson, *Selected Essays*, p. 181.
21. I have in mind Edward Weston and Paul Strand. Weston's *Daybooks* abound with statements that echo transcendentalism.
22. *Miscellanies*, No.124, HGT, p. 75f.
23. See *Images or Shadows of Divine Things, by Jonathan Edwards*, ed. Perry Miller (New Haven: Yale University Press, 1948), No.

25, p. 49.
24. Edwards worked out the idea of the "new spiritual sense" most thoroughly in his *Treatise Concerning Religious Affections*, ed. John Smith; *The Works of Jonathan Edwards*, Vol. 2 (New Haven: Yale University Press, 1959). See Part III, First Sign.
25. "The Mind," No. 62, *HGT*, p. 64; *WEA*, p. 380.
26. "The Mind," No. 45, *HGT*, p. 47; *WEA*, p. 362.
27. "The Mind," No. 1, *HGT*, p. 25; *WEA*, p. 336.
28. The distinction appears in Miscellany No. 123, for example, and is fundamental to No. 782, an entry closely related to the *Treatise Concerning Religious Affections*. See *HGT*, pp. 245f., 113ff.
29. "The Mind," No.66, *HGT*, p. 66; *WEA*, p. 383; also Miscellany No. 238, *HGT*, p. 247.
30. *Miscellanies*, No. 94, "Trinity"; *HGT*, p. 256.
31. *Miscellanies*, No. 94, "Happiness"; *HGT*, p. 128f. Also, "The Mind," No. 1, *HGT*, p. 27; *WEA*, p. 338.
32. *Miscellanies*, No. 87. Also, cf. note number 4 above.
33. "The Mind." No. 63, *HGT*, p. 65; *WEA*, p. 382.
34. See note number 1 above.
35. *Treatiese Concerning Religious Affections*, p. 205.
36. *Religious Affections*, p. 201.

Second Lecture

"KNOW THYSELF!"
SAMUEL TAYLOR COLERIDGE'S SCIENCE OF LIVING WORDS

Truth is compared in scripture to a steaming fountain; if her waters flow not in perpetual progression, they stagnate into a muddy pool of conformity and tradition. 1

Introduction

EXPERIENCE teaches us that many an enterprise, large or small, consumes its own vitality, so that there follows upon an initial season of growth, expansion, and fruitfulness a time of contraction and hardening. The history of countless nobly inspired revolutionary parties repeats this lesson year by year. Revivals in literature, art, and philosophy obey the same tendency, though at a somewhat slower pace. Religious reformations that re-invigorate (and purify) ancient rites and infuse overfamiliar scripture with a widening and liberating spirit lapse into complacent and unyielding orthodoxies. Religious change, in fact, seems to be particularly susceptible to this law of thwarted progression. The reformations that began in the sixteenth century in Europe at first energized the spirit and the intellect; but then they hardened into new scholasticisms as arid and brittle as those that had gone before. Religious reforms appear to be destined to generate within themselves their own opposing spirit, the spirit of dogmatism. Dogmatism is the uncritical clinging to creeds and practices of the past. Uncritical here means that which is merely habitual and hence unleavened by fresh reflection. Dogmatism, therefore, is any habitual way in which mind and spirit proceed (in science, politics, or religion) that is not regularly subjected to new scrutiny and judgment. The human propensity to dogmatism permits authorities, such as clergy, public officials, and "experts" of various sorts to pursue inherited and unconsidered patterns of thought and conduct in the midst of a pliant and acquiescent citizenry.

In his timelessly fresh essay, "What is Enlightenment?" (1784), Immanuel Kant characterized the spiritual weakness dogmatism fosters in his exclamation: "It is so comfortable to linger in tutelage to others."[2] It is so easy to allow others to supervise us and think for us. There is no antidote to this complacency except to muster courage and resolve to use our own powers of reasoning and use them, moreover, in public. "Dare to know!" "Dare to be wise!" This ancient admonition, which Kant borrowed from the poet Horace and placed in the preamble of his essay, is a fitting epigraph for all the critical, inquiring spirits who have determined not to permit others to remain as the custodians of their own intelligence and conscience. Enlightenment, therefore, is the moral and spiritual process of going forth—and of growing up—out of bondage to others.

With respect to religious thought, Kant offered as trenchant a critcism of dogmatism as has ever been put before the public. Moreover he recognized the general method that the self-determining religious intelligence henceforth would have to adopt. No longer would it be sufficient merely to appeal to scripture. Religious thinking would have also to make trial of itself by employing the tests it carries within itself—pre-eminently the test of moral experience. Kant also perceived that clericalism and the control of religion by political authority block the way to such freedom and authenticity. In short, he was a prophet of the 19th century revitalization of religion, a revitalization that amounted to a revolution and that is sometimes called the romantic revolution in religion. But by personal disposition as well as social circumstance he could not himself venture far in the direction in which he pointed. Such venturing fell to others, mainly of succeeding generations, better equipped by sympathy, insight, experience, and opportunity. And among these others none is a more remarkable individual than Samuel Taylor Coleridge.

1. Coleridge as Explorer of Self

Coleridge is becoming better known today, perhaps than he ever was, save to his most intimate friends and family members. This better knowledge of him is arising in a striking renaissance of Coleridge scholarship, exemplified in a number of exceptionally fine studies of recent date. And certainly a paramount power in this renaissance is the incomparable skill and erudition that Professor Kathleen Coburn has been investing in the editing of Coleridge's voluminous and often astonishing notebooks. Students of Coleridge will require years fully to assimilate and to interpret the range and dimensions of the man that are now being newly revealed. Even so, it is certain, Coleridge will always be known first and foremost to the public as one of the genuinely original poets of the English language—chiefly as the author of "The Rime of the Ancient Mariner," "Kubla Khan," and "Christabel"—and as the originator of a theory of poetry and of criticism that steadily continues to command close attention. His influence however, encompasses more than his poetry and criticism. As philosopher and theologian of culture and society, for example, he has affected not only the 19th century but the 20th as well. T. S. Eliot's essay, *The Idea of a Christian Society* (1939), attests to that fact, for it acknowledges the inspiration Eliot drew from the last book Coleridge himself sent to the press, *On the Constitution of the Church and State, According to the Idea of Each.*

Like his contemporary in Germany, Friedrich Schleiermacher, who was also a counterpart in many respects in the romantic "revolution" in religion, Coleridge contributed to the life of his nation as a whole, although, unlike Schleiermacher, he held no post in either church or university. By his large circle of friends and acquaintances and his correspondence with them as well as by his famous powers of conversation, by his journal essays and articles on politics, trade, religion, and other matters of public importance, by his public lectures on literature, philosophy, and current affairs, as well as by his poetry and such books as his literary biography (*Biographia Literaria*) published in 1817, Coleridge made himself a citizen of his age. These facts of his life are relatively well known, and also that he was very closely associated with William and Dorothy Wordsworth, that he was unhappily married, and that throughout the years he had to struggle with poor health and addiction to opium, an addiction which developed from his taking of laudanum as medicine.

What is less well known, in the present at any rate, is that Coleridge was a principal agent in bringing to English and American religious thought the liberality of spirit and critical quality of reflection that Kant had extolled in his essay, "What Is Enlightenment?" and had succinctly recommended in his declaration that it is the duty of thinking persons not only to think for the sake of the public but to think in the open forum of the public. Coleridge, however, coupled the independence of inquiry Kant praised with a clarity of empirical observation and a psychological acuity that combined to create an unusual wisdom founded in experiential self-knowledge. These traits endowed him with a natural authority and created for him an audience that facility in critical philosophizing alone could not have gathered.

Coleridge was in fact possessed by a genius for self-knowledge, a genius that was authentically daemonic —and hence exacted much from him—and prepared him in a special and painful way to impart vitality to religious thinking again. Most of what follows in the paragraphs to come is an examination of the theme of self-knowledge in Coleridge'a writings and notes; but it is appropriate here to anticipate some of its characteristics.

i) First of all, Coleridge experienced words as themselves *beings*, as *things* and not as mere signs or artificial conventions. This experience is perhaps indispensable to any poet of stature, but it affected Coleridge with an unusual forcefulness. Indeed, words were for him powers that beckoned or even compelled his ever-observing intelligence to move across and beyond the thresholds of everyday awareness; they could grasp him "as with a hand of flesh and blood" and make him gaze upon features of experience not customarily acknowledged in consciousness.

ii) Hence, and this is the second characteristic of his self-knowing to be emphasized, the conventionally definite—often all too definite—boundaries between the seen and the unseen, the palpable and the merely "fanciful," were not so definite for him; and this is exemplified in the fact that Coleridge could not meekly follow Kant, even though he acknowledged that the German philosopher "took possession of [him] as with a giant's hand," where the latter drew broad and heavy lines, meant to be ineffaceable, between genuine intuitions of sense and spurious intuitions of faith inspired by what he dismissed as *Schwärmerei* or undisciplined private enthusiasm.

iii) A third element in Coleridge's endeavor to acquire self-knowledge was his persistent effort to "desynonymize" words habitually used interchangeably for the purpose of gaining what he called distinctness of consciousness: consciousness of shadings and contrasts of meaning in words generally treated as simple equivalents and of variations of shape and tone in the continuum of experience that are ordinarily overlooked.[3]

One effect of Coleridge's direct acquaintance with the liveliness of words and of his conviction of the necessity of distinctness of consciousness was to awaken others to the fact of the animative energy of language and to the thick manifoldness of the reality it symbolizes. Among Coleridge's American disciples was the influential preacher and theologian, Horace Bushnell, who attested to the effect of Coleridge's *Aids to Reflection* on him. "My habit before [prolonged study of the *Aids*] was only a landscape," Bushnell wrote in a letter.[4]

Now I saw enough to convince me of a whole other world somewhere overhead, a range of realities in higher tier, that I must climb after, and, if possible apprehend. ... In this mood or exigency, I discovered how language built on physical images is itself two stories high, and is, in fact, an outfit for a double range of uses.

The eye of Coleridge's imagination roved in a "perpetual systaltic movement" between the outer world and the inner world of self, discovering ever fresh analogies between the two.[5] Like the voyager he portrayed in his poem, "The Rime of the Ancient Mariner," he became conscious of the spirits that moved in him "nine fathoms deep," and this consciousness of the deeps of his being made him an agonist in the sense of that word which Miguel de Unamuno has more recently taught us to respect. He not only as a poet wrestled with philosophy; as a striving believer he wrestled with doubt; as a profound doubter he wrestled with dread and was familiar with more than intellectual scepticism. Like Augustine, he knew of the abyss on which the soul opens and of what William James called "the momentary discrepancy" between sanity and madness and of what he himself described as the "sacred horror" of existence: "Not TO BE ... is impossible: TO BE, incomprehensible."[6] One of Victorian England's chief preachers and theologians, Frederick Denison Maurice, speaks for many when he wrote to Coleridge's son, Derwent, concerning his father's *Aids To Reflection* that he did not know of any volume "with more clear tokens and evidences" that the author in speaking of spiritual conflict and of what is needful to the support of our being spoke only of that with which he himself was directly familiar.[7] Something of this essential authenticity of Coleridge's spirit conveys itself in one of the aphorisms appearing early in the *Aids*, having to do with the painfulness of sincere reflection[8]:

> In countries enlightened by the gospel ... the most formidable and (it is to be feared) the most frequent impediment to men's turning inwards upon themselves, is that they are afraid of what they shall find there. There is an aching hollowness in the bosom, a dark cold speck at the heart, an obscure and boding sense of somewhat, that must be kept out of sight of the conscience; some secret lodger, whom they can neither resolve to eject or retain.

When Coleridge admonished his readers he was also admonishing himself; and this aphorism gives us one, though not all, of the reasons why he became utterly convinced that[9]

> there is one knowledge, which it is every man's interest and duty to acquire, namely self-knowledge: or to what end was man alone, of all animals, endued by the Creator with the faculty of self-consciousness? Truly said the Pagan moralist, "from heaven descended [the maxim] 'Know thyself!'"

Through his own experienc Coleridge had won the hardearned wisdom that if we do not practice the duty of self-knowledge, we become content with a meager substitute for true happiness or well-being. We become content with the mere absence of pain and with numbness of spirit, which is a state sadly inferior to that true health and vitality for which our nature is formed. "Know thyself" was, therefore, an imperative Coleridge believed to be binding on all. It is also a personal aspiration which the reader sees running as a motif throughout Coleridge's notes, essays and books. Coleridge's modulations of this theme introduce us directly to his vigilant examination of the human nature that is subject to this duty. In teaching himself and others to heed the maxim "Know thyself!" he communicated to English and American religious thinking new liveliness and inspired it to value more highly its own intrinsic freedom.

2. Self-Knowledge: "To know is a verb active."

Initially self-knowledge appears as a noble ideal that Coleridge enjoins. This enjoinment occurs in lines of his composition which came into print as incorporations into Robert Southey's "Joan of Arc, An Epic Poem," published in 1796.[10]

> That we may learn with young unwounded ken
> Things from their shadow. *Know thyself my Soul!*

However, self-knowledge acquired for Coleridge a wider and deeper import than these lines by themselves might prompt us to suspect. Later on, in *The Friend*, on which he labored first as a journal and subsequently as a book, Coleridge wrote that "whatever is conscious Self-knowledge is reason."[11] This direct association of consciousness, self-knowledge, and Reason is important for what is still to come in our effort to interpret Coleridge, and we need therefore to dwell a little on it.

The statement stands in a context occupied with the distinction "in kind" between Reason and Understanding. (Here we have an important instance of his interest to increase distinctness of consciousness by desynonymizing words habitually used interchangeably.) Coleridge stresses this distinction also in the *Biographia Literaria*, where he writes that the main object of *The Friend* was to establish the distinction, as well as in *The Statesman's Manual* and in *Aids To Reflection*. It would be satisfying to spend much time and space tracing the full significance of this distinction in Coleridge's writings over-all, but here we have to confine ourselves to a brief characterization of the most essential differences he draws between Reason and Understanding.[12] Understanding is the name (always capitalized, like Reason) Coleridge reserves for the "faculty" of mind that associates the phenomena or appearances it receives through the senses. It *arranges* and *generalizes* upon these phenomena according to rules of experience. Reason, on the other hand, *perceives*; it perceives ideas—ideas in the sense that Plato accorded the word—that is, eternal forms, and it grasps these timeless, spiritual realities directly; at least, that is the proper work to which Reason is devoted. Reason, then, has a perceptual or intuitive character; it is analogous to the bodily senses except that it is an organ of spiritual sense directed to spiritual objects. Reason, furthermore, grounds and stabilizes Understanding, taking up the generalizations Understanding makes and transforming them into intuitively indubitable truths. Hence, Understanding is discursive;

Reason is intuitive. Understanding, moreover, is turned outward, and it is foreshadowed in insects and animals as instinct. Reason, on the other hand, sets human being apart from all other creaturely being. And, as the statement "whatever is conscious Self-knowledge is Reason" implies, it has the character of self-consciousness. It always illuminates the self, even when turned toward something outward, toward something haveing the quality of "outness" (to use a word that Coleridge found especially appealing).[13] But Reason may also be turned directly inward, as an organ of self-intuition.[14] Hence, the employment of Reason, or Reasoning, always illuminates the self because, as Coleridge liked to repeat in words borrowed from Milton: "Reason is [the soul's] being." Therefore, Reason, in the special sense Coleridge attaches to it, is ever present in his mind when he speaks of self-knowledge.

Even more emphatically, the twelfth chapter of the *Biographia Literaria* (a chapter that has become trampled ground from much tedious disputation on the unprofitable topic of its author's indebtedness to his German philosophical cousins) declares that as geometry begins with postulates, so does philosophy, and [15]

> [the] postulate of philosophy and at the same time the test of philosophical capacity, is no other than the heaven descended KNOW THYSELF! . . . And this at once practically and speculatively.

Consequently, when in 1825 Coleridge announces that "there is one knowledge, which it is every man's interest and duty to acquire, namely self knowledge," and makes that interest and duty the main subject of his book, *Aids To Reflection*, the reader who has carefully followed

Coleridge's thinking throughout the years is well apprised that Coleridge is addressing a fact with which all of the kinds of his experience, as poet, as critic, as essayist, and as philosopher of consciousness and imagination, have consisitently confronted him.

Much of the force of Coleridge's postulate and test of philosophic capacity "Know thyself!" lies in the thoroughly active sense that verb *know* bears. "To know is in its very essence a verb active." So runs one of the most crucial statements in the twelfth chapter of *Biographia Literaria*.[16] That knowing is an act is one of the primary articles of Coleridge's philosophical creed; and we should accord to it the greatest importance. However, we can better appreciate why it is so laden with significance for Coleridge, if we take notice of his account of his long philosophical pilgrimage, one that began in his adolescence, for he was a tremendous reader from his schoolboy days. For a period of time, Coleridge tells us, he subscribed to a philosophy of knowledge, which he particularly admired in the form to which David Hartley (1705-1757) had adapted it, that maintains that the "ideas" in our minds are "impressions" made there by objects conveyed to them by the senses. (As one would expect from what we have already learned about Coleridge's later distinction between Reason and Understanding and the Platonic meaning that the word "idea" bears within that distinction, Coleridge came to reject this Hartleyan usage of "idea.") Moreover, according to this philosophy of Coleridge's youthful years, these "ideas" are connected or "associated" by certain fixed principles: successiveness in time, nearness in space, interdependence or cause-effect relation, likeness, difference, and so forth. Hence, the mind's "ideas" or "impressions" form an "order" that reflects the "order" in which objects impinge upon it, insofar as they sensibly affect the mind. Associationism in this form represents the mind as a kind of apparatus recording motions or impulses (much as a sensitized tape records electronically translated sounds) initiated by the action of the outer world upon our organs of sentience, our sight, our hearing, our touch, etc.

The reason why Coleridge came to reject Hartley's empiricism is clear. He asked, in effect, why may we not justly call such an "order" in the mind a "confusion"? Or, a "delirium"? If, for example, we suppose that "likeness" of qualities, such as color or shape, or succession in time govern our minds, what is to stop our attention, when we stand atop some height and survey the scene spread around us, from being rushed from one impression of red to the next and the next, or from one tree-shape to other like shapes, or from being compelled to "zig-zag" helplessly from color to shape to texture until the mind becomes a "shoreless chaos" of passive associations?[17] Coleridge criticized Hartley's philosophy because it ascribes to the mind *passivity* only; it subjects the mind to "the despotism of outward impressions"; it turns the self that knows into a "mere quick-silver plating behind a looking-glass," "a lazy Looker-on on an external World."[18]

"Delirium" and "despotism of outward impressions" are strong characterizations of the psychological import of Hartley's philosophy. Nevertheless, Coleridge never used words carelessly. Hence, before we move on, we should think about their significance, especially in connection with Coleridge's exceptional "irritability" or what we today would call his sensitivity. He was unusually responsive to the stimulae of the senses. This trait of his constitution, combined with his well developed analytical powers, contributed to making him not merely a keen observer on occasion but an individual who could scarcely help but be aware: aware not only of the gross and large but also of the more elusive changes in motions and qualities taking place in his environment as well as within himself. And his conviction that it is our duty to attain to ever greater distinctness of consciousness was of a piece with this heightened awareness. Readers familiar with "The Rime of the Ancient Mariner" may recall that among the several threads unifying that ballad poem of an ocean voyage, one of the most striking is the play of vivid and dramatically interacting colors. The play of color is essential to the whole symbolic meaning of the ballad. The poem is the work of one who wrote with a painter's eye. J. A. W. Heffernan maintains that in Coleridge, as in his contemporaries the landscape painters John Constable and J. M. W. Turner, a distinctive and new perception of color emerges, a perception that is sensitive to the ways in which colors modify each other and hence to their infinite variability.[19] Here we need only turn to Coleridge's notebooks for abundant evidence of his acuity in attention and of his power to describe vividly and precisely. There is an entry for the year 1804, written in the Lake District, which well exemplifies what page after page exhibits.[20]

In the River that runs into Rydale all the sides were bright as bright could be with the celestial yellow green of the western Sky in Spring & Summer, before Stormy nights/the color of a part of the Rainbow/it thinned & breadthened in obedience to the Breeze—after dinner we had a glorious View out of the window, of the Lake/our View was isthmused by T. Ashburner's. Yew Tree between us & the Lake/ on the one side of this we saw the Lake that same celestial Yellow Green, & on the other a divine mulberry-puce color occasioned by a blood-Cloud.

This passage shows Coleridge the observer to have been truly *at work* in his observing. His account of the colors and forms in his view of the river-running-into-the-lake is the product not of passive registrations of impresssions upon the blank tablet of the mind but of active attending, discriminating, and organizing of the elements of the rich, dense manifold presenting itself. What we see here of Coleridge as notebook-keeper is closely related to what we know of Coleridge as a poet who was fully aware that patient and accurate observation are indispensable to the making of a true poem. This is a point he reiterates in his *Biographia Literaria*.[21] And patience, as he wrote elsewhere, is an *act* of intellect or of self, not to be confused with passivity;[22] accuracy similarly bespeaks voluntary effort or intellectual action. If we use Coleridge's own language to describe what he was about in making this journal entry, then we might say that as a painter quickly makes a water-color sketch as a preparatory note for a carefully composed landscape, so Coleridge in rapid fashion sets down a verbal sketch of the scene he views, a sketch or note on which he can someday draw for a poem. But a final product, such as a poem, should be an *imitation*, not a *copy*. (Again,, Coleridge desynonymizes words ordinarily used interchangeably.)[23] To imitate means, in Coleridge's philosophy, to re-create nature or things observed in their livingness, and whoever would imitate must be able to perceive the living fount of nature (*natura naturans*) in the garment of appearances (*natura naturata*) that life-creative wears. Moreover, life-creative always issues in dynamic polar oppositions: heat and cold, dryness and moisture, motion and rest, colors at counter ends of the spectrum, and so forth. Hence, Coleridge's verbal sketch pays close attention to the living oppostions in the view, such as the colors yellow-green, purple-brown (mulberry-puce), and blood red, the lake and the sky, the motion of the river and the stillness of the framing shapes of the window and yew tree; and he draws these polarities forward, into relief, by introducing associated memory images of dark stormy nights and rainbows. Observation of this order—observation that leads into imitation—requires the *act* of imagining.

We will return to Coleridge's idea of imagining further along. Here it is important to recognize that he abandoned Hartley's philosophy, and the general tradition of John Locke as he had come to understand it, not because he thought sense perception to be unimportant but because he knew it to be so important that he also knew he required other principles than those of associationism to explain it. In fact Coleridge never did surrender the essential truth that empiricism affirms, namely, that the mind depends upon sense perception. (Locke, he said, took half the truth for the whole truth.) But he went beyond conventional empiricism, or empiricism conventionally interpreted, to the point of asserting that the entire intellect engages in the act of perceiving.

Undoubtedly Coleridge's conviction that "to know is a verb active" and that true perception is properly an act within the action of Reason was greatly strengthened by another kind of experience familiar to him. For he was keenly conscious that sensations and images can live independently in the mind, as it were, while Reason is drowsing, and produce real delirium as well as nightmares (or "nightmairs," as he called them).[24] He suffered from them chronically, and turned those sufferings into the poem, "The Pains of Sleep." "Horrors of every night," he wrote of the shapes and thoughts which tortured him in sleep, "—I truly dread to sleep/it is no shadow with me, but substantial Misery foot-thick." And he went on in the same vein: "[My] dreams [have become] the Substances of my Life."[25] This confusing of dreams with substance in sleep is terrifying enough in itself; but Coleridge also recognized it as symbolical of the many sorts of failure of self-knowledge that occur over a wide range of states of consciousness that are imperfectly developed and less than full self-consciousness. From his susceptibility to sensations and images ungoverned and unorganized by Reason Coleridge inferred what a real hell must be like: conscious madness.[26] To be sentient without at the same time *Reasoning* in one's sentiency is to experience chaos.

3. Self-Knowledge: Intelligence as a Self-Development

Coleridge's conviction that "to know is a verb active" ramifies deep and far in his consideration of consciousness and of the nature of self. Chapter XII of *Biographia Literaria* shows him tracing these ramifications, although the form in which he there presents his argument, as a chain of ten sequential theses, is stiff and cumbersome, and he later voiced dissatisfaction with it. Characteristically, the argument is in part subordinated to the status of a footnote, and it is also entangled with polemic against Descartes' famous refutation of scepticism: "I think, therefore I am." Nevertheless, Coleridge's central conviction and contention is relatively clear, and it is with this central conviction that we are concerned, not with the ill-suited sequence of theses. The conviction Coleridge sets forth, the conviction that becomes a pivotal position, is that self is act. We will do better, however, to put it in a more expanded statement: Self, symbolized in the act of declaring "I am," is act. Here we should note, in order the better to follow Coleridge's progression of thought, that he uses the terms spirit, self, self-consciousness, and even intelligence as all being expressive of the same reality: the act symbolized in "I am."[27] And we could just as well add Reason and will to this list. Consequently, alternative and complementary ways of stating the same pivotal position are: Spirit is act; self-consciousness is act; Reason is act. We can identify the steps Coleridge takes that lead to this postion in the following way: i) The action of Reasoning—for we will use Reasoning here to encompass thinking, knowing, and so forth—is not a mere predicate of self. Reasoning, as Coleridge puts it, is not a quality "supervening to a substance." ii) Rather, Reasoning is one with the being of the self. iii) Hence, if we accept that to reason is to act, then we are led also to accept that the very existence of the self has the essential character of act.[28] This position is so important that we can scarcely emphasize it strongly enough: The act of reasoning, of which we are directly aware in reasoning, is one with the act of existing as a self. This is an immediate truth. It is not, however, a truth we come by casually; it must be earned by the exercise of philosophical imagination, by "self-intuition"; but once it is earned, its validity remains self-evident. Later in the century, Gerard Manley Hopkins employed the word *selves* as a verb, and this seems to be consonant with Coleridge's idea of self.[29] Consequently, borrowing from Hopkins to interpret Coleridge, we may say: *reasoning is selving*.

The principle that self is act is an anchor that moors much of what else Coleridge has to say about self, self-knowledge, and self-consciousness. When, for example, still in Chapter XII of *Biographia Literaria*, Coleridge adds that intelligence is power,[30] and elsewhere asserts that Reason is power,[31] he is enlarging—in a most significant way—on the meaning of the principle that self is act. Indeed, this conception of intelligence and Reason as power is also primary in his whole philosophy of self and self-consciousness. In fact, Coleridge regards the principle that Reason is power as one of the indestructible truths that Plato taught. (A corollary of this truth is that ideas are eternal laws, eternal patterns of energy, that regulate, inform, and empower the mind.) Self-consciousness and Reason are, then, dynamic. That which is act is dynamic-act. "I am by the law of my nature a reasoner," Coleridge says; and, he goes on: "My mind is energic—I don't mean energetic."[32] The distinction he implies is evidently the distinction between allowing that mind *resembles* energy and holding that mind *is* energy or, more precisely, a species of energy.

Coleridge expands the principle that self is act still further. Self-consciousness and Reason are not only energic, not only kinds of power; they are developmental. He writes, for example, that intelligence reveals itself "in the process of self-construction"; that "intelligence is a self-development."[33] The meaning of phrases such as these is that the self which is act and power is also processive, capable of growth. Whether we direct our attention to self as thinking and knowing, or to self as intelligence or to self as self-consciousness or to self as will, we are attending to that particular kind of act that exhibits the character of a life-process, a growth-process. But in addition—and this again is a momentous further qualification of all that Coleridge has said or implied already —what distinguishes self-consciousness or Reason from all other kinds of processive growth or development is that it must direct itself. It must assume responsibility for governing its own evolution. For Coleridge the terms spirit and will most suitably convey this dimension of selfhood.

The analogies Coleridge uses—which we may also call symbols—to bring into relief the developmental, evolutionary character of Reason are often drawn from the sphere of vegetative and insect life. One of the most striking is that of the growth and metamorphosis of the caterpillar into the butterfly. It is no surprise that he gives a detailed account of this process in his notebooks.[34] But the application of the process as symbolic of development of self appears in his *Biographia Literaria* at the point at which he is speaking of the philosophic imagination, one of the modalities of Reason. As the wings of the butterfly form within the skin of the caterpillar, he observes, so the "sacred power of self-intuition" forms within us all, though not all exercise it; and it appears first in our moral experience, in our desire of happiness and in our pangs of conscience.[35]

It is evident in all that we have learned from Coleridge's statements about self and Reason as act and from his choice of qualifying words and analogies or symbols that *self-knowledge* and *self-intuition* must be taken as verbal nouns. It is with self-knowing that he is concerned. Self-knowing is a process in which we who look upon or know ourselves are the very looking and knowing process itself. And as we know, as we reflect, we change, we develop, or evolve. Consequently, we can take Coleridge's statement, "I am by the law of my nature a reasoner," and paraphrase it in the following way: "I am by the very law of my nature self-directing reasoning process." The Reason that is the soul's very being is free act. Hence, "[We] *must* either rise or sink."[36]

4. The Evolving Self

When in his *Aids To Reflection* Coleridge admonishes the reader to heed the maxim "Know thyself!" he envisions the self to which he directs attention not as a discrete, solitary self but as a living being or, better, a living process of becoming that is analogous to the crocus in the field, which develops roots, stem, leaves, petals, pistil, and stamen by attracting life from the surrounding soil, air, and moisture. The crocus becomes what it is to be by developing out of an antecedent harmony, out of "an antecedent unity" of life, a cause that is prior to it and also immanent in it as its productive power.[37] The self, however, develops in the context not only of nature but of "the great community of persons" the context of history; and so it draws its energy from a larger antecedent web of life. There is, of course, another decisive difference between self and the kind of living, developmental process which the crocus represents. The crocus receives its principle of growth as an endowment from nature. The self, however, must discover its true law and adopt that law for itself. It must oversee itself. More than that, the self as spirit draws its life not only from the created order but from infinite Spirit. The spirit that is self, Coleridge writes,[38]

> cannot originally be finite . . . it can be conceived neither as infinite nor as finite exclusively, but as the most original union of both. In the existence, in the reconciling, and the recurrence of this contradiction consists the process and the mystery of production and life.

The world of life from which and toward which every self proceeds is a world that is more than *this* world. To live, to reason, to reflect is to become, to "selve" within an eternal plan or providence.

Coleridge quarrelled with the extreme Augustinian doctrine of predestination, which deprives human being of its freedom. For this reason he rejected Jonathan Edwards' theology, though how much he knew of Edwards is open to question. But he did not quarrel with the doctrine of election; indeed, he regarded Paul's Epistle to the Romans (the *locus classicus* of that doctrine) as "the most profound work in existence."[39] Coleridge characterized the immanent effect of election in langauage of which Edwards would have thoroughly approved: it is the experiencing of "the stream of grace in [our] hearts, though [we] see not the fountain whence it flows, nor the ocean into which it returns."[40] However, the discernment of this stream of grace constitutes a moral and a religious task, a task that must be executed in the freedom of which we can be deprived only by ourselves. The motto Coleridge wrote on the lintel of the *Aids To Reflection* is "Self-super-intendence!", a motto that echoes Kant's exhortation, "Dare to know!" "Dare to be wise!" "Have the courage to reason for yourselves!" But to superintend ourselves we must discover the perfect law, the Logos, the Word that infuses and suffuses us with light and life. It is for this reason that, in the Preface to the *Aids*, the author writes that his first object is to teach the reader "the value of the science of words," to which he immediately adds that he means the science of "living words."[41] "Living words" are different from *mere* words or names or images, more, that is, than words employed as arbitrary signs. "Living words" are vehicles of the invisible presence and power of that which they "name."[42] "Living words" impart life. They are the "wheels of the intellect," Coleridge adds, referring to the prophet Ezekiel's vision, by the river Chebar, of the wheels in which was the spirit of life. "Living words," then, are vessels of spirit and life that bear up the human spirit and enable it to mount to the door of the house of the Lord.[43] Without such "wheels" our Reason cannot develop or evolve. They impart to each self the antecedent unity of life from which it has proceeded. As we continue to investigate Coleridge's "science of living words" we learn a good deal of what he means by symbol.

5   Symbols as Living Words

We have already taken notice of Coleridge's statement that the mystery of production and life is the reconciling of the contradiction that the self or spirit "can be conceived neither as infinite nor as finite exclusively, but as the most original union of both." Now we need to add and then to unfold the fact that symbols are a principal means by which this contradiction is reconciled and the original union of the infinite and the finite made alive again in each self that strives to become a truly living soul.

Coleridge's philsophy of symbol is scattered here and there and is gathered together in no one place, although *The Statesman's Manual* and *Aids To Reflection* have much to offer us as we attempt to recover the tenor and direction of this thinking. He provides definitions of symbol in both of these publications. The better known of these occurs in *The Statesman's Manual*, where he contrasts symbol with allegory. An allegory, Coleridge declares, is "but a translation of abstract notions into a picture langauge...."[44]

> On the other hand a Symbol ... is characterized by a translucence of the Special in the Individual or of the General in the Especial or of the Universal in the General. Above all by the translucence of the Eternal through and in the Temporal. It always partakes of the Reality which it renders intelligible; and while it enunciates the whole,

abides itself as a living part in that Unity, of which it is the representative.

In the *Aids To Reflection*, he is briefer, though the context in which the definition appears is worth attention for its own sake. It is a long footnote—so characteristic of Coleridge!—on the subject of the interpretation of Genesis I and II in which he asks: Why should not these chapters be both symbol and history at once? "Or rather how could it be otherwise? Must not of necessity the first man be a symbol of mankind in the fullest force of the word[?]"[45]

> [S]ymbol, rightly defined [is] a sign included in the idea which it represents;—that is, an actual part chosen to represent the whole, as a lip with a chin prominent is a symbol of man.

Any phenomenon or fact of nature and history may act as a symbol, be it the butterfly emerging from its chrysalis, a mythic and/or historical person, or a vibrant prophetic word, such as that of Micah: "What does the Lord require of thee, but to do justly and to love mercy."

Before we attempt to track Coleridge's idea of symbol further, however, it will be useful to get some immediate impression of the intimacy he felt and perceived in the relation between symbol and Reason or self-knowledge. This perception appears in a notebook entry, often quoted, dated Saturday night, April 14th, 1805.[46]

> In looking at objects of Nature while I am thinking, as at yonder moon dim-glimmering thro' the dewy window-pane, I seem rather to be seeking, as it were *asking*, a symbolical language for something within me that already and forever exists,

than observing any thing new. Even when that latter is the case, yet still I have always an obscure feeling as if that new phaenomenon were the dim Awaking of a forgotten or hidden Truth of my inner Nature/It is still interesting as a Word, a Symbol! It is λογος, the Creator!<and the Evolver!>

It would be difficult to find anything more eloquent or illustrative of Coleridge's philosophy of symbol than this paragraph. Among the many facets it exhibits, what we need especially to notice for our purposes is the effect in himself that Coleridge describes as the product of his perception of the "moon dimglimmering thro' the window-pane." The effect is the feeling of awaking to a forgotten truth. No passage outside of Coleridge's poetry better exemplifies his distinctive empirical Platonism or Platonic empiricism than this expression of a sense of being recalled to something inward and forgotten by a definite phenomenon that is at the same time for him "a Word, a Symbol," a phenomenon that is also Logos.

This April experience of being brought to the threshold of a forgotten life anticipates what Coleridge writes later in his periodical, *The Friend*, and repeats in his literary biography concerning the poet and the poem of genius. Such genuis, he observes, has the capacity to restore to the world the lustre that custom has "bedimmed."[47]

> To find no contradiction in the union of the old and the new; to contemplate the Ancient of days and all his works with feelings as fresh, as if all had then sprang forth at the first creative fiat; characterizes the mind that feels the riddle of the

universe, and may help unveil it.

The notebook entry together with the later comment on the poet and poem of genius help us to see what Coleridge means when in the *Aids To Reflection* he speaks of the language of Scriptures as exhibiting "the conspiration of the divine with the human" spirit.[48] The living spirit that breathes in the symbolical language of Scripture performs the mental refreshment which Coleridge has earlier attributed to the genius of the poet. The process of awaking that the symbol initiates is the process of rejoining the self to its spiritual origins, to the antecedent unity from which every self proceeds. Now, however, in the *Aids To Reflection* Coleridge is dwelling on more than the need to rekindle the sensations of childhood (the capacity he so much admired in Wordsworth); he is rather speaking of the need each self experiences of recollecting its spiritual birthday.

Coleridge's idea of symbol is, of course, intertwined with his theory of imagination, although he continues to meditate on symbol after he gives up theorizing about imagination. Much has been written about his philosophy of imagination; we shall not attempt to follow out that pholosophy here but only to stress three facts in his exposition of imagination as a mode of intuitive, organizing Reason. Even before setting out these facts, however, it should be made clear that the premise of this brief excursion into Coleridge's idea of imagination is that it makes little sense to divide perception, Understanding, imagination, and Reason into separate organs of intellect; Coleridge himself makes this quite clear.[49]

Imagination is, according to the famous passage in *Biographia Literaria*, "the living Power and prime Agent of all human perception ... a repetition in the finite mind of the eternal act of creation in the infinite I AM." The poet consciously and voluntarily employs this imagination in a second degree to dissolve and diffuse what such perception offers and then to unify again. Hence, imagination, or Reason as imagining, gives us perceptual access to phenomena in all of their "outness" and enables us to incorporate them into ourselves, perhaps then to make a poem or to read a poem, to paint a picture or to understand the picture already painted by repeating the artist's creative process. i) The first fact in Coleridge's theory of imagination to be stressed here is that imagination brings to light what is there; it is the power by which phenomena appear to us in their undimmed lustre. (By its etymology the word *fancy* or *phantasy* makes this point more clearly than does the word *imagination*.)[50] ii) The second fact is that imagination is the capacity to dissolve and re-unify, providing us with the power to create. iii) The third fact of Coleridge's theory, which we need to allow its full weight in our interpretation of the meaning of Coleridge's maxim, "Know thyself!" is that imagination unites sense and Reason, enabling us to perceive, think, and reflect symbolically. It incorporates "the Reason in Images of the Sense," and organizes the "flux of the Senses" by the "self-encircling energies" or ideas of Reason.[51] When, consequently, we apprehend an object such as the moon and value it as a fleeting incarnation of an eternal law or idea, we are perceiving and thinking as imagining beings; we are symbolizing. Indeed, according to Coleridge, we have access to ideas solely in their symbolical forms, as imagination, our "true inward Creatrix," gives them to us.[52] "An idea, in the highest sense of that word, cannot be conveyed but by a *symbol*."[53]

There is a famous passage in "The Rime of the Ancient Mariner," which illustrates the point. In the gloss on lines 263-266, Coleridge writes of the becalmed and tormented Mariner:

> In his loneliness and fixedness he yearneth towards the journeying Moon, and the stars that still sojourn, yet still move onward; and everywhere the blue sky belongs to them, and is their appointed rest, and their native country and their own natural homes, which they enter unannounced, as lords that are certainly expected and yet there is a silent joy at their arrival.

The "journeying Moon" here is a symbol of the idea of the homeward bound wanderer, the pilgrim moving toward the celestial city, the exile being repatriated, the prodigal son returning to the feast, the fallen soul being re-united with its source. This is a universal idea or true idea and law informing Bible, myth, literature, art, and daily experience alike. The Mariner is no philosopher, but his consciousness is heightened and made more distinct by his yearning sight of the moving moon. His "weary eye" is refreshed; his parched tongue is loosened to bless the fearsome creatures of the deep and to pray. All nature, according to Coleridge, is to the religious person "the art of God," and the spirit of nature "discourses to us by symbols."[54] As it has been for so many others throughout the ages, for Coleridge also nature is a second book of revelation; but it is a revelation through symbols.[55] The Bible is the first such book, first, that is, in degree. With its histories of individuals and corporate personalities it is "a system of symbols," which the imagination interprets. In that sense, it is legitimately called "*the* WORD OF GOD," presenting to us, as it does, "the stream of time continuous as Life and a symbol of Eternity."[56] But to interpret either or both of these books profitably, we have to advance into that self-knowledge which leads us to recognize that we are dependent on symbols. Hence, both Bible and nature counsel: "Know thyself!" The effort to comprehend the science of symbols prompts us to seek knowledge of self; in entering into ourselves we grow in the knowledge that truth proffers itself to us in symbols that are living words.

Hence the making of poetry and the study of nature both require proficiency in the learning of the language of symbols. No less does the religious undertaking to reflect. Reflection is a looking down into self, symbolized "in the endeavor to see the reflected image of a star in the water at the bottom of a well."[57] The *Aids To Reflection* is filled with such analogies and symbols as this. It proceeds from level to level by employing the very method Coleridge wishes to communicate: in looking down we can extend our range and acquire greater keenness of vision only by incorporating into our Reason images of sense. The whole movement of the *Aids* is dialectical or—as Coleridge would put it—"centrifugal and centripetal." The reader moves outward toward nature and history, to fix attention upon objects and facts and then returns inward to invest these objects and facts with the energy of thought until they become luminescent focal points in which the reader's experience is clarified. This is the method of "the voluntary reproduction in our minds of those states of consciousness or . . . those inward experiences, to which . . . the teacher of moral or religious truth refers us."[58] Coleridge no longer uses the term imagination in the *Aids*. Reflection has come to take its place. But the process of reflection is similar to that of imagination. It entails two moments: 1) the striving for distinctness of apprehension by attending to particulars; ii) the incorporation of these particulars into oneself, thereby enlarging self-consciousness. Hence, reflection with the aid of symbols and with much effort and often pain issues in a deepening and an expansion of self. It is, in effect, a process of self-recreation. With each increment of growth, new knowledge becomes possible: knowledge of self and of the unity of life to which every self belongs.[59] But this process of self-recreation can be sustained only with the co-inspiring Spirit. Something of the nature of this progression is conveyed in passages of *Confessions of an Inquiring Spirit* (a series of letters Coleridge wrote on the authority of Scripture, published, however, only after his death), in which he speaks of the Bible as "a breathing organism," an organism that inspirits life into the reader. In the reading of the Bible, while "the Spirit beareth witness with our spirit," the "unsubstantial, insulated Self passes away," to make room for the larger life the Scripture communicates in symbols. In these letters, Coleridge compares the relation of his Reason to the Scripture to the relation of the moon to the solar radiance.[60] Reason reflects this Light; this Light refracts itself to Reason in symbols.

The duty of self-knowledge leads into an unending spiral motion toward an ultimate re-union with the living and substantial truths, now apprehended darkly, that are encompassed in the eternal Logos. A thematizing symbol Coleridge employs in the *Aids* is that of the stranger, the sojourner, the pilgrim. Perhaps no passage in the book is more lovely than the comment on Aphorism XXII in the "Introductory Aphorisms," where Coleridge is writing that it is our duty and in our interests to form the habit of reflection, "for an unreflecting Christian walks in twilight among snares and pitfalls."[61]

> We are next to bring out the divine portrait itself, the distinct features of its countenance, as a sojourner among men; its benign aspect turned towards its fellow-pilgrims, the extended arm, and the hand that blesseth and healeth.

We are, by reflection, to form more distinctly in our self-consciousness the image of the creator-Logos which inwardly accompanies us on our toilsome way. The figure of the pilgrim appears soon again, described as one who sets out before the sun has risen and is frightened and confused by the "phantasms" of sleep. "The shapes of the recent dreams become a mould for the objects in the distance, and these again give an outwardness and sensation of reality to the shapings of the dream."[62] This pilgrim symbolizes the still indistinct but awaking self-consciousness, the soul struggling out of its drowsed ignorance. In the "Conclusion" of the book, Coleridge alludes once more to this figure, in the course of attacking his old adversary, the philosophy of associationism that takes words to be mere names or arbitrary signs only. In rebuttal, Coleridge writes: "*My words*, said Christ, *are spirit*." Christ used "words and names," Coleridge goes on to say, "that designate the familiar yet most important objects of sense . . . water, flesh, blood, birth, bread! But he used them in senses, that could not without absurdity be supposed to respect the mere *phaenomena* . . ." He used them, rather, as living words, as symbols. To understand them otherwise is to understand them discursively only, to glide over them or run them through the mind. That is to evade their meaning, but it is an evasion to which the drowsed soul is unconsciously addicted. "And this awful recalling of the drowsed soul from the dreams and phantom world of sensuality to *actual* reality,—how has it been evaded!"[63] Progress in self-knowledge is hard, yet to shun it is to remain a stranger at home.

Coleridge made an entry in his notebooks that bears directly on the utter necessity of symbol to the mind that would be whole.[64]

> All minds must think by some *symbols*—the strongest minds possess the most vivid Symbols in the Imagination—yet this ingenerates a want [a need] . . . for vividness of Symbol: which something that is without, that has the property of *Outness* . . . can alone gratify/even that not fully. . . . I say, every generous mind . . . feels its *Halfness*—it cannot *think* without a symbol—neither can it *live* without something that is to be at once its Symbol, & its *other half* . . . .

This entry provides a fitting epigraph not only for Coleridge's own but for all reflection aspiring to true self-knowledge. The intelligence developing itself and endeavoring to become generous cannot live without its "Other half," namely, vivid and vivifying symbols.

NOTES

1. *The Notebooks of Samuel Taylor Coleridge*, ed. Kathleen Coburn, 3 volumes to date (Volumes I & II, New York: Pantheon Books, 1957, 1961; Volume III, Princeton: Princeton University Press, 1973), Vol. I, No. 119. Hereafter cited as Notebooks, together with volume and entry numbers.
2. Immanuel Kant, "What Is Enlightenment?" in *Critique of Practical Reason and Other Writings in Moral Philosophy*, trans. L. W. Beck (Chicago: University of Chicago Press, 1950), p. 287.
3. Notebooks, III, 3312; see also *Biographia Literaria*, ed. J. Shawcross, 2 volumes (London: Oxford University Press, 1954), Vol. I, pp. 61, 109. Hereafter cited as BL with volume and page numbers.
4. *Life and Letters of Horace Bushnell* [ed., Mary Bushnell Cheney] (New York: Harper & Brothers, 1880), p. 209.
5. The phrase "perpetual systaltic movement" is Professor Kathleen Coburn's. See *Experience into Thought: Perspectives in the Coleridge Notebooks* (Toronto: University of Toronto Press, 1979), p. 66. Professor Coburn uses this phrase to describe the Mariner, but I believe it fits Coleridge as well. Professor Coburn also attributes to Coleridge the coining of the word *subconsciousness*; see *The Self Conscious Imagination: A Study of the Coleridge notebooks in celebration of the bi-centenary of his birth 21 October 1772* (London: Oxford University Press, 1974), p. 21.
6. *The Friend*, ed. Barbara E. Rooke, 2 volumes; *The Collected Works of Samuel Taylor Coleridge* (Princeton: Princeton University Press, 1969), Vol. I, p. 514. Hereafter cited as The Friend, (CC), together with volume and page numbers.
7. Frederick Denison Maurice, "Dedication to the Rev. Derwent Coleridge," Appendix in *The Kingdom of Christ*, ed. A. R. Vidler, 2 volumes (London: S. C. M. Press, Ltd., 1958), Vol. II, p. 355.
8. *Aids To Reflection*: With a preliminary essay by James Marsh, ed. H. N. Coleridge (Burlington, Vermont: Chauncey Goodrich, 1840), Aphorism XIX, p. 75. Hereafter cited as AR with the aphorism number and page number.

9. AR, "Preface," p. 64.
10. *The Complete Poetical Works of Samuel Taylor Coleridge*, ed. E. H. Coleridge, 2 volumes (Oxford: At the Clarendon Press, 1912), Vol. I, p. 132n. Emphasis added.
11. The Friend, (CC), I, 156.
12. See especially The Friend, (CC), I, 154ff. and AR, VIII, pp. 250ff.
13. Notebooks, III, 3325.
14. BL, II, 167.
15. BL, I, 173.
16. BL, I, 180.
17. BL, I, 77, 225f.
18. BL, I, 82; and *Collected Letters of Samuel Taylor Coleridge*, ed. E. L. Griggs, 6 volumes (Oxford: At the Claredon Press, rev. ed., 1966), Vol. II, p. 709. Hereafter cited as Collected Letters with volume and page numbers.
19. James A. W. Heffernan, "The English Romantic Perception of Color," in *Images of Romanticism*, ed. K. Kroeber and W. Walling (New Haven: Yale University Press, 1978), p. 137f.
20. Notebooks, I, 1812.
21. BL, I, 59; II, 5.
22. "Essay on Faith, "in *The Literary Remains of Samuel Taylor Coleridge*, ed. H. N. Coleridge; *The Complete Works of S. T. Coleridge, in seven volumes*, ed. Shedd (New York: Harper & Brothers, 1854), Vol. V, p. 558.
23. BL, II, 56; and "On Poesy or Art" in BL, II, 255ff.
24. Notebooks, III, 4046.
25. Collected Letters, II, 982, 1009.
26. *Specimens of the Table Talk of Samuel Taylor Coleridge*, ed. H. N. Coleridge; *The Complete Works of S. T. Coleridge, in seven volumes*, ed. Shedd (New York: Harper & others, 1854), Vol. VI, p. 349. Hereafter cited as TT together with page number.
27. BL, I, 183.
28. Chapter XII of *Biographia Literaria* addresses several issues. This paragraph represents my own summary interpretation of one of the lines of thinking Coleridge pursues there.
29. The reference is to the poem by Hopkins, "As kingfishers catch

fire, dragonflies draw flame."
30. BL, I, 188, 198.
31. TT, 336.
32. TT, 503.
33. BL, I, 188.
34. Notebooks, I, 1378.
35. BL, I, 167.
36. BL, I, 167.
37. AR, Aphorism VI, pp. 106ff.
38. BL, I, 185.
39. TT, 458.
40. AR, Aphorism V, p. 103.
41. AR, "Preface," p. 62f.
42. AR, Aphorism VIII, pp. 218ff. and notes; see also TT, 313.
43. Ezekiel 1:15ff.; 10:15ff.
44. *The Statesman's Manual* in *Lay Sermons*, ed. R. J. White; *The Collected Works of Samuel Taylor Coleridge* (Princeton: Princeton University Press, 1972), p. 30. Hereafter cited as SM, (CC), together with page number.
45. AR, "Reflections introductory to Aphorism X," p. 243n.
46. Notebooks, II, 2546.
47. BL, I, 59.
48. AR, Aphorism XIV, p. 121f.
49. SM, (CC), Appendices C & E; see also Owen Barfield, *What Coleridge Thought* (Middletown, Connecticut: Wesleyan University Press, 1971), pp. 96f., 219.
50. Fancy or fantasy derives from the Greek verb, *phantazein*, to make visible.
51. SM, (CC), 29.
52. Notebooks, III, 4046.
53. BL, I, 100.
54. "On Poesy or Art" in BL, II, 254, 259.
55. SM, (CC), Appendix C, 70.
56. SM, (CC), 28f.
57. AR, Aphorism XXIII, p. 79n.
58. AR, Aphorism VIII, p. 69n.
59. *Quantum sumus, scimus* [As much as we are, so much we

know]. See AR, Aphorism XXIII, p. 79n. and SM, (CC), 78.
60. *Confessions of an Inquiring Spirit* in *The Literary Remains of Samuel Taylor Coleridge*, ed. H. N. Coleridge; *The Complete Works of S. T. Coleridge, in seven volumes*, ed. Shedd (New York: Harper & Brothers, 1854), Vol. V., pp. 591, 622, 580.
61. AR, Aphorism XXII, p. 78; see also "Comment" on Aphorism XIX, p. 76.
62. AR, Aphorism XXIX, pp. 82f.
63. AR, "Conclusion," p. 349.
64. Notebooks, III, 3325.

Third Lecture

WILLIAM JAMES' METAPHYSICS OF RELIGIOUS EXPERIENCE

Introduction

WILLIAM James delivered his Gifford Lectures, *The Varieties of Religious Experience*, more than three quarters of a century ago, in 1901 and 1902. Calling the lectures "A Study in Human Nature," he notified his audience in Edinburgh that he addressed them neither as a theologian, nor as historian of religion, nor as anthropologist and that he came to the task in hand from his own earlier labors in psychology. However, readers opening James' book now, in the 1980s, can proceed no more than a few chapters before realizing James' identification of himself as a psychologist, significant as that fact is, scarcely prepares them for the distinctiveness and abiding liveliness of his treatment of religious experience, undisfigured by any mark of pedantry. The character of the book obviously owes more to James' own unique intelligence and character than it does to the rules and conventions of this or that academic discipline, though this is not wholly surprising since James was as much an innovator in psychology as he was in philosophy.

The distinctiveness of *The Varieties* comes partly from James' stated intention to present for analysis and interpretation materials readily accessible to all. He called the evidences he had collected *documents humains*, that is, living words of flesh and blood men and women, evidences not hidden from public view but ready to be gathered by any and all who frequent the "beaten highways" of history. James' contribution was to be to set these testimonies of religious experience in a newly instructive order and context. A second reason for the distinctiveness of James' treatment is that he elected to attend to religion in its developed and mature forms. The opening lecture of *The Varieties* makes clear that James firmly declined to interpret religion by taking the early circumstances of the appearance of religion, be those circumstances historical or biological, as the key to the meaning of religion. But the feature of James' approach to religious experience that is most noteworthy of all—the feature that is really fundamental to the two kinds of distinctiveness already mentioned—is the obvious presence in his inquiry of a spirit open and humane yet independent and critical. As a seasoned and reflective psychologist James was fully aware that psychological investigation has its own integrity. But James was a philosopher also, although at the time of the Gifford Lectures his greatest philosophical works were still to be written. He knew well, therefore, that any psychological inquiry into human nature carries within itself broad philosophical assumptions and raises philosophical issues of equal scope, which psychology alone is not competent to resolve. One of the notable merits of *The Varieties of Religious Experience* is that it treats the intersections of psychology and philosophy with candor and circumspection and always keeps the reader informed about the premises with which its author is working.

Since the beginning of this century many others have engaged in the interpretation of religious experience. At the present moment history of religion and anthropology of religion enjoy a special popularity and prestige. At the same time, both psychology of religion and philosophy of religion have changed profoundly since James' day. In many instances the academic interpretation of religion has become highly technical and even recondite to the point that the non-specialist can scarcely expect to wrest much profit from them. As a consequence of these developments, there is today among scholarly interpreters of religion nothing even remotely resembling a school of Jamesians active on our scene. James' influence, to be sure, remains. It is even significant; but it works for the most part in a transmuted form and indirectly through the mediation, for example, of Alfred North Whitehead, who owed to James a large intellectual debt.

Nevertheless, *The Varieties* itself lives on. Indeed, it thrives—with all the vigor of an achievement that changing intellectual fashions cannot diminish. Still today, as eighty years ago, it expands the reader's world with its author's unusual breadth of sane intelligence and range of human sympathy. It is a book truly for the public.

James' range of sympathy and capacity to identify himself with others appears most dramatically in the fact that he made *The Varieties* a virtual library of first-hand accounts of religious experience and, in particular, of conversions and mystical ecstasies and raptures. Nothing else on the subject rivals it for its wealth of autobiographical narrative. To immerse oneself in the book is to enter a region densely populated by vivid personalities all of whom have compelling stories to tell of the momentous events that have befallen them and changed the course of their lives. James drew upon the personal testimonies of such as Augustine of Hippo, Teresa of Avila,

George Fox, John Bunyan, Leo Tolstoy and of hundreds of other men and women, famous and little known, from the early centuries of the Christian era down to the very times at which he was writing his lectures. He even included accounts of his own extra-normal experiences, although he disguised them so that they are not immediately identifiable as his own. It is this combination of exceptional diversity and autobiographical authenticity that does so much to enthrall the newcomer to the book. At the same time, however, this teeming variety together with the fervor and intensity that many of the testimonies exhibit may also have the effect of overwhelming the reader. Persons not yet familiar with James' goals and his ways of proceeding in the book are apt to confess, from the very midst of the case histories which the author has gathered, that what they desire above all else is a terse and abstract definition of religion. They want a concept or an idea which will deliver them from the bewildering profusion of energetic, excited religious emotions that threaten to resurrect themselves from the very page. But these traits are essential to the book's character. They belong part and parcel to James' fundamental intention.

1. James' Goals and Procedures in *The Varieties*

Two remarks James made in letters composed close to the time of his lectures in Edinburgh help us to understand his goals and methods. The first of them, written in April of 1900, was addressed to Frances Morse, a lifelong friend.[1]

The problem I have set myself is a hard one: *first*, to defend (against all the prejudices of my "class") "experience" against "philosophy" as being the real backbone of the world's religious life—I mean prayer, guidance, and all that sort of thing immediately and privately felt, as against high and noble general views of our destiny and the world's meaning; and *second*, to make the hearer or reader believe, what I myself invincibly do believe, that, although all the special manifestations of religion may have been absurd (I mean its creeds and theories), yet the life of it as a whole is mankind's most important function. A task wellnigh impossible, I fear.[2]

This privately declared manifesto, "to defend 'experience' against 'philosophy,'" signals one of the most important features of James' intellectual creed: the conviction that individual religious acts and experiences precede general theory in authority. Of course the principle is itself a philosophical principle. Its reciprocal is that theory validates itself only if it succeeds in illuminationg personally felt or attested experience. These convictions express an attitude that pervades all of James' philosophizing; and while he gave them greater elaboration as the years passed on, he was already allowing them free play in *The Varieties of Religious Experience*.

The very title of James' lectures is symbolic of his goals and his procedures. Hence, the feature that can bewilder us in our initial readings of the book, its profusion of first-hand accounts of urgent and peremptory religious experiences, was central to James' intention to underscore the differences we meet with in religiousness. "The theorizing mind," James observed, "tends always to the oversimplification of its materials."[2] He was very much aware that our dependence on language as the chief instrument of thinking easily disposes us to assume that whatever we can fashion with our abstractive discourse into a single idea must somehow reflect an actual unity latent in the welter of our experience. James put his readers on guard against that assumption, and warned that "we may very likely find no one essence, but many characters which may alternately be equally important to religion."[3] He proceeded then to define religon—in a chapter he quite characteristically titled "Circumscription of the Topic"—in a highly flexible way as follows:[4]

> the feelings, acts, and experiences of individual men in their solitude, so far as they apprehend themselves to stand in relation to whatever they may consider the divine.

The need for so elastic a definition of religion becomes even clearer as one reads further and encounters the so widely differing sorts of religious personality that James encompassed under the broad rubrics of the "healthy-minded" and the "sick soul." Not only are the temperaments of these groups dissimilar; their experiences are so diverse as to imply quite different life-worlds and hence conflicting metaphysical convictions. To the "healthy-minded" evil is a muted reality at most, while to the "sick soul" it is a stark reality that cannot be expunged. Such divergent qualities of experience portned very different ideas of the nature of the divine. As James made the transition in his lectures from his account of the "healthy-minded" to his detailed portrait of the "sick soul," he commented on the significance of such profoundly divergent qualities of experience:[5]

Here we have the interesting notion fairly and

squarely presented to us, of there being elements of the universe which may make no rational whole in conjunction with the other elements, and which, from the point of view of any system which those other elements make up, can only be considered as so much irrelevance and accident—so much "dirt," as it were, and matter out of place.

Once again, this comment symbolizes much of James' philosophic attitude and more especially his distinctive empiricism, which prompted him to urge that unlikeness and unrelatedness are as important features of our experiential world as are similarity and connection. Certainly, James did not hold that the religious experiences of different kinds of individuals are so utterly unlike one another that they altogether resist comparison, making up only a meaningless aggregate of particulars. But he did believe them to be too varied to be reduced to a single essence. Hence the idea of religion that James patiently developed from his *documents humains* was calculated to reckon as seriously with diversiy as with sameness. This intellectual stance sets him at a considerable distance from all those who postulate a single, self-identical essence of religion within its apparently heterogeneous manifestations, from Friedrich Schleiermacher down to Mircea Eliade.

The second remark James made that comments on his goals and method bears on the fact that many of the personal religious testimonies he quoted, often at some length, are extreme in their intensity. Some of James' early readers were shocked by the abundance of confessions from persons evidently subject to exceptional and even abnormal spiritual excitement. But James explained to one of his correspondents, Edwin D. Starbuck, in 1904 that he could not hope to study religion to advantage by examining it in its average manifestations only.[6] It would never do to study the passion of love [by] examples of ordinary liking or friendly affection, or that of homicidal [anger by] examples of our ordinary impatiences with our [fellows]. So here it must be that the extreme examples let us more deeply into the secrets of the religious life, explain why the tamer [people] value their religion so much, tame though it be, because it is so continuous with a so much [more acute] ideal.

A typical example of this exaggerated spiritual excitement occurs in the personal narrative of the Quaker pioneer George Fox.[7]

As I was walking with several friends, I lifted up my head, and saw three steeple-house spires, and they struck at my life. I asked them what place that was? They said, Lichfield. Immediately the word of the Lord came to me, that I must go thither. . . . Then was I commanded by the Lord to pull off my shoes. I stood still, for it was winter: but the word of the Lord was like a fire in me. So I put off my shoes. . . . Then I walked on about a mile, and as soon as I was got within the city, the word of the Lord came to me again, saying: Cry, "Woe, to the bloody city of Lichfield!" So I went up and down the streets, crying with a loud voice, Wo to the bloody city of Lichfield. . . . As I went thus crying through the streets, there seemed to me to be a channel of

> blood running down the streets, and the marketplace appeared like a pool of blood. When I had declared what was upon me, and felt myself clear, I went out of the town in peace. . . . After this a deep consideration came upon me, for what reason I should be sent to cry against that city, and call it. The bloody city!. . . . But afterwards I came to understand, that in the Emperor Diocletian's time a thousand Christians were martyred in Lichfield. So I was to go, without my shoes, through the channel of their blood . . . that I might raise up the memorial of the blood of those martyrs, which had been shed above a thousand years before.

George Fox and similar eccentric figures give us access, James explained, to "pattern-setting" religion, to religion welling up, as it were, out of extraordinary persons at a high temperature or energy level and communicating its energy to others. It was his quest of "original experiences" in "pattern-setters," then, that led James to populate the pages of his book with so many startling personalities. "Those experiences," he added,[8]

> We can only find in individuals for whom religion exists not as a dull habit, but as an acute fever rather. But such individuals are "geniuses" in the religious line; and like many other geniuses . . . have often shown symptoms of nervous instability.

What we further learn from James concerning these typical or exceptional persons, as we look back at them from the vantage of the conclusion of the book, is that they often exemplify as well quite another quality than heightened excitement; they exemplify an expansion of the scope of perception, a breaching of the dikes of ordinary awareness so that a much wider field of consciousness flows in. Such a visionary experience as befell George Fox often overcomes prophets.

James' decision to focus attention on "original" and "pattern-setting" religious experience had much to do with the impression his book made on his contemporaries and still shapes our own responses to his interpretation of religion. James studied medicine as a young man, and since that science regards what is abnormal or pathological as especially instructive, James may well have developed his predilection for the unconventional religious personality partly as a consequence of that passage in his education. The decision also reflects his profession as a psychologist, but of equal importance to it were the crystallizing principles of his philosophy, and his temperament as well. We may be helped further in our understanding of the general metaphysical principles present in *The Varieties of Religious Experience* if we attend to a few other elements that appear to bear on James' choice of the individual as the focus of his work.

2. James' "Individualism"

We know that James considered institutional religion with its public symbolism, its rituals and theology, to be of little value in comparison with the testimonies of exceptional religious personalities. Part of the reason for this judgment about theology is that it afforded him far less insight into the living heart of so much of religion, into the fact of strife and struggle. Church or dogmatic theologies and systematic theologies, in particular, tend to wear the appearance of slick philosophical theism. They present at their centers an idea of God that verges toward monism or idealism, which are ways of thinking that of logical necessity mute the starkness of evil and therefore fail to reflect the intensity of personal warfare with satanic powers or demons of despair. Popular or practical theism, on the other hand, the kind of faith that actually energizes individuals in their hours of need, is more frankly polytheistic or at least pluralistic; it does not so consistently attempt to deny the metaphysical reality of the evil that afflicts indivuduals.[9] Hence, James regarded institutional theology as less candid, as less adequate, to the facts of experience.

Moreover, James felt a great sympathy with persons for whom life is a contest. He himself had to contend with poor health much of his life. It was on his health's account that he gave up his medical studies and—years later—had to prepare much of his Gifford Lectures while bedridden. This condition made him acquainted with melancholy and despair and with the cost of keeping one's spirit strong while the body sinks in weariness. Therefore, he could appreciate what is required to fight courageously without assurance of the outcome. And he must have heeded the undeniable voice of his own experience in coming to the conviction that the sources of courage are not within institutions and their patterns but in much deeper regions to which the soul alone has access. In any case, James had reason to admire the valiant in heart, and as he made utterly plain in his later publication, *Pragmatism*, he felt it incumbent on himself to declare unequivocally that defeat and irretrievable loss are experienced realities that no official creed or academic philosophy can expunge.[10]

At the same time, James was himself nearly as complex as the materials he had gathered for his lectures, and his own temperament also showed a strong strain of optimism, an optimism of the kind that is willing to be put to the proof. The American 19th century was as varied and contradictory as any century of modern times; but—among other things—it was the century of the gospel of self-reliance, preached by Ralph Waldo Emerson and advocated by countless others. This gospel meant to turn the moral and religious energies of the people toward the future and resolutely away from the past and from the institutions and social habits in which the past preserved itself. Optimism and individual self-confidence were virtually sacred duties; Henry David Thoreau stated this faith in brash and now familiar words:[11]

> I have lived some thirty years on this planet, and I have yet to hear the first syllable of valuable or even earnest advice from my seniors. They have told me nothing, and probably cannot tell me anything, to the purpose. Here is life, an experiment to a great extent untried by me.... But man's capacities have never been measured; nor are we to judge of what he can do by any precedents, so little has been tried. Whatever have been thy failures hitherto, "be not afflicted, my child, for who shall assign to thee what thou hast left undone?"

Thoreau's exclamation, "Here is life, an experiment to a great extent untried," resonates with a tone James could affirm. The heroes of the present age who open hopeful pathways into the future are not venerable social bodies recollecting and refurbishing the ideas of by-gone times but venturesome individuals who think forwards as they live forwards. Emerson, whom James respected, addressed the students of Harvard Divinity School in 1838 urging them to test and to try for themselves.[12]

> Truly speaking, it is not instruction, but provocation, that I can receive from another soul. What he announces, I must find true in me, or reject; and on his word, or as his second, be who he may, I can accept nothing.

Religious truth, Emerson admonished his audience, "cannot be received at second hand." And in the opening sentences of his book *Nature* he wrote to similar effect:[13]

> The foregoing generations beheld God and nature face to face; we through their eyes. Why should not we also enjoy an original relation to the universe?

It was for such original relations to the universe that James looked among the testimonies he had collected for his book, setting aside whatever bore the appearance of "second-hand religious life." Although he indulged neither in Thoreau's brashness nor in Emerson's round oratory, he did conduct his own thinking by the same general principle they praised. He had, of course, made it entirely his own principle; and as he pondered the labors spent on *The Varieties of Religious Experience*, he confirmed that he himself had travelled forever beyond Christian orthodoxy. To his correspondent, Henry W. Rankin, he wrote in the summer of 1901:[14]

> Now, at the end of this first course [of lectures], I

feel my "matter" taking firmer shape, and . . . I believe myself to be (probably) permanently incapable of believing the Christian scheme of vicarious salvation, and [am] wedded to a more continuously evolutionary mode of thought.

This declaration that he could not make "the Christian scheme of vicarious salvation" an article of his own faith is a particular instance of James' general principle that only original religious experience carries convincing authority. Salvation cannot be ours by virtue of creedal assurance that another has procured it for us. Rather, salvation can be ours only insofar as we ourselves experience it in the act. More than that, however, James also often admitted, both in *The Varieties* and elsewhere, to a standing disenchantment with *all* orthodoxies, whether they be religious, philosophical or scientific; and we may take that inclusive disenchantment with orthodoxy as such to be still another manifestation of his constitutional preference for what Emerson called "an original relation to the universe." But James' distrust of theological orthodoxy in particular had another contributory cause; it grew as well from his suspicion that institutional or school theologies—"scholastic" theologies both medieval and modern—seek to appease our human hunger for original or personal relations to the universe with a diet of speculative generalities and semant qualifications. All of this becomes unmistakably clear in the 18th of the Gifford Lectures, the one entitled "Philosophy," where James dwelt at length on the pragmatic or practical barrenness of the labors of scholastic theologians and asked:[15]

What is their deduction of metaphysical attributes but a shuffling and matching of pedantic dictionary adjectives, aloof from morals, aloof from human needs, something that might be worked out fom the mere word "God" by one of those logical machines of wood and brass which recent ingenuity has contrived as well as by a man of flesh and blood.[?]

Despite statements of this order, we would be wrong to take James' attitude toward theology as negative without qualification. He did admire, for example, the kind of theology that excels in descriptive accuracy concerning the affective states of the soul; and he could concede that elaborate "systems" of theology might well satisfy an authentic esthetic need of the religiously devout intelligence. Nevertheless, whatever partial agreement with this or that theology on this or that particular point James might discover, at least one fundamental objection of a religious sort always kept him at a distance; it was the objection that theology always slights or else wholly ignores the reality of evil.

Systematically stringent theology, what James called "philosophical theism," is in fact often open to this criticism. But James' perception of the issue doubtlessly was also directly affected by the ideas of his contemporary, Josiah Royce. Royce was both a colleague and a friend of James and also the foremost American philosopher to attempt to represent Christianity as a religious version of philosophical idealism. James engaged in a long debate with Royce, and as the years passed he disagreed ever more profoundly with Royce's position that the eternal would lack perfection or the perfection of the eternal would in fact be defective if there were not evil present in the temporal order. James called such statements "guileless thoroughfed" thinking, thinking that deals with shadows, while those who "live and feel know truth."[16] This last remark is bitter and telling. It reveals the root of James' distrust of conventional thinking about matters of religion, while it also points us again to his strong preference for direct testimony concerning religious experience from individuals. The efforts of theology, whether the theology in question be that of the medieval scholastic or the 19th-century idealist, to demonstrate a particular quality of God, such as the goodness of God, by showing that it is a logical property of the idea of God as perfect, are efforts that simply miss the point. The goodness of God certainly arises as a problem, but not because there is something amiss merely *within* the philosophical-theological system. It arises as a problem in the lived and felt facts of human experience, which make up a real world that such systems do not so much as recognize. The lived and felt facts of our experience, according to James, materialize in the recesses of our personal being, where our sense of worth abides. If, for example, we think of Job's friends as theologians, we see that they scarcely addressed the felt reality of Job's suffering. Thinking of this kind, which is so utterly insensible to the "pinch" of reality, to personal experience, James called ratiocination. In his vocabulary ratiocination means calculative or computative thinking, impersonal thinking, thinking with mere symbols at a high level of generality. Thomas Aquinas or Josiah Royce, like other ratiocinators, weave nets out of ideas and general categories, but these nets are too coarse to catch real religious facts. Real religious facts simply flow through such nets. The scholastic theologian might well reply to James that if theology cannot capture the quarry James regarded as so important, then the conclusion must be that James has misjudged what is important. But James came to the writing of *The Varieties of Religious Experience* with a different set of convictions. Facts that are systematically ignored by impersonal thinking are nonetheless fact. Religious experience and feeling, like personal suffering, are real facts belonging to a real world. "Compared with this world of living individualized feelings," James wrote, "the world of generalized objects which the intellect contemplates is without solidity or life."[17] According to James, then, religion deals with facts that come into being in the deeps of the soul of the individual.

3. James' Map of Religious Experience

In drawing a map of human experience, James located the springs of religion in a region that the conventional psychology of his day regarded as too volatile and elusive to yield significant knowledge: in the region of feelings. A brief reference to James' own psychology may help us here, for perhaps nothing else that James gave to the world exceeded in importance and suggestiveness his description and analysis of consciousness as a "stream." He contended that such metaphors as "chain" or "train of consciousness" do not appropriately characterize consciousness. Consciousness as it really appears to us, he said, "is nothing jointed; it flows. A 'river' or a 'stream' are metaphors by which it is most naturally described."

When we take a general view of the wonderful

stream of our consciousness, what strikes us first is the different pace of its parts. Like a bird's life, it seems to be an alternation of flights and perchings. The rhythm of language expresses this, where every thought is expressed in a sentence, and every sentence closed by a period. The resting-places are usually occupied by sensorial imaginations of some sort, whose peculiarity is that they can be held before that mind for an indefinite time, and contemplated without changing; the places of flight are filled with thoughts of relations, static or dynamic, that for the most part obtain between the matters contemplated in the periods of comparative rest.

What James otherwise named the "substantive parts" of conciousness he also called its "perchings," and what he otherwise, in more conventional language, designated as its "transitive parts" he also called its "flights." For our purposes we should take particular note of these "transitive parts" of "flight," since what they reveal about consciousness as James apprehended it is unusually important. They reveal consciousness as being in significant measure a flow of feelings—a flow that is often swift or even headlong—connecting the "perchings" or larger objects of our thinking, that is, our images and ideas. It is this flow of feeling that furnishes consciousness with its continuity. These metaphors which James so carefully chose tell us how strongly he believed consciousness to be a process. Moreover, as he asserted, our personal sense of identity depends on these transitive, connective feelings. Our most intimate sense of self lies in mental activities, swift as flight, which we can scarcely arrest long enough to contemplate.

James brought this view of consciousness as being like a stream to his lectures on religious experience. He explained to his audience in Edinburgh that we may have an idea—in the language of his psychology, we may contemplate an idea when our thinking "perches"—that refers to an object of grand, almost infinite proportions. It could be, for example, an idea of cosmic space. But the contemplation of this idea is one thing. The cosmic space to which the idea refers is another. The cosmic space is not ours; it is only the contemplation of cosmic space that is ours, that belongs to our "stream" of thinking or consciousness. On the other hand, he continued, our inner state, the "stream" of consciousness, "is our very experience itself; its reality and our experience are one."[19] The import of this observation is that cosmic space as a generalized idea, taken by itself, is an abstraction, an idea plucked out of the stream. The full reality to which it belongs is something much denser, much swifter, and much more complex than the abstracted idea when taken alone suggests. The full reality is the idea together with the "stream" or, as he also calls it, the "field of consciousness." James then proceeded to condense this developed philosophical psychology of consciousness into a brief statement in *The Varieties* that is critical to our understanding of his interpretaion of religious experience.[20]

> A conscious field *plus* its object as felt or thought of *plus* an attitude towards the object *plus* the sense of self to whom the attitude belongs—such a concrete bit of personal experience may be a small bit, but it is a solid bit as long as it lasts;

not hollow, not a mere abstract element of experience, such as an "object" is when taken alone. It is a *full* fact, even though it be an insignificant fact; it is of the *kind* to which all realities whatsoever must belong; the motor currents of the world run through the like of it; it is on the line connecting real events with real events.

Religious experience is compounded of such small bits of personal experience. It also involves a conscious field *plus* a felt object *plus* an attitude *plus* the sense of self. We apprehend religious experience, that is, religion coming into existence in experience, at the intersection where the encircling "world" and our streaming consciousness join. It is in these intersections that "facts" become solid or real. Our sense of reality shows many different shades of intensity. But it is most intense where it is connected with our sense of self and of personal destiny. And this sense abides in the deeps of our personal individuality. James went on to elaborate this point in the following words:[21]

> Individuality is founded in feeling; and the recesses of feeling, the darker, blinder strata of character, are the only places in the world in which we catch real fact in the making, and directly perceive how events happen, and how work is actually done.

Hence religion in the making appears in the transitive moments of consciousness, in the feelings that bear preeminently on our sense of self and personal destiny. James' metaphysics of religious experience is also a metaphysics of personal individuality and its relations to the world that environs it. In addition, it is a metaphysics of knowledge, for that which is most real is what we know most directly and intimately. Now, since reality and direct knowledge coalesce in the deeps of individual personal existence, original religion is far removed from public or generalized symbols.

These convictions and principles have much to do with James' particular interest in religious conversion and mysticism. Not unnaturally, James' own personal sympathies also prompted him to give conversion and mysticism his careful attention. Two years after he had completed the Gifford Lectures, he wrote to James Henry Leuba that he was devoid of "God-consciousness in the directer and stronger sense,"[22]

> yet there is *something in me* which *makes response* when I hear utterances made from that lead by others. I recognize the deeper voice. Something tells me, *"thither lies truth"*—and I am *sure* it is not old theistic habits and prejudices of infancy. Those are Christian; and I have grown . . . out of Christianity. . . Call this, if you like, my mystical *germ*. It is a very common germ. It creates the rank and file of believers.

Indeed, had James not been receptive at some level to the testimonies of converts and ecstatics, it is unlikely that he would have spent so much effort in his inquiries into religion. However, it is with James' principles for the interpretation of conversion and mystical experience that we must here concern ourselves. And to follow his analysis of these two kinds of experience, we need to return briefly to his general conception of religion.

As we have already noticed, he held religion to be a constellation of feelings, acts, and experiences. His psychological approach ascribed particular importance to the feeling elements. Yet no single feeling can be the essence of religion. Instead, religion is distinguished by a number of characteristics. James underscored the following traits. (1) Religious feeling is responsive to the divine. James made no effort to use a theological definition of the divine. It may be personal or impersonal; it may imagined as a "world-soul" as Emerson would have it. But James did stress that an authentically religious attitude intuits or apprehends the divine as being active; "gods are conceived to be first things in the way of being and power. They overarch and envelop, and from them there is no escape."[23] (2) In the second place, sincerely religious feeling excludes the attitude of grumbling and complaint. Whatever else religion may be, then, it is a response to the divine or god-like that is solemn and that neither curses nor jests at the world. (3) A third characteristic is awareness that tragedy is afoot in the world and lies in wait for all of us, whatever our pretensions to moral heroism. "The sanest and best of us are of one clay with lunatics and prison inmates, and death finally runs the robustest of us down. And whenever we feel this . . . all our morality appears but as a plaster hiding a sore it can never cure."[24] (4) The fourth quality of religious feeling James emphasized—and it is perhaps the most critical of all—appears in the fact that the religious temper is *intense* and *energetic;* it includes a sense of vitality coming to us from outside the perimeter of our normal consciousness and inducing in us a mood of welcome ranging from cheerful serenity to enthusiastic gladness. More than that, a religious experience, when it is an "acute fever," leads us to be careless and forgetful of ourselves. Then we shut our mouths and are content to be "as nothing in the floods and waterspouts of God. In this state of mind . . . the hour of our moral death has turned into our spiritual birthday."[25] We can gather all of these characteristics of religion in the following summary statements: religion as responsiveness to the godlike is solemn yet glad; it includes a tragic sense of life but holds this tragic sense in suspension in a higher mood of enthusiastic assent and carelessness of self. In a remark that echoes his letter to Frances Morse, James added that religion "becomes an essential organ of our life," performing a necessary function that "no other portion of our nature can so successfully fulfill."[26]

James' stress on the intensification of energy and mood that religion fosters prepares us for the strong interest he shows in conversion and mysticism. The convert and the mystic are typically energized individuals, and, of course, they answer to James' preference for personalities excited by what he called "original" religious experience. Furthermore, they are likely to show an enhanced sense of identity, a greater liveliness of feeling, through which "the motor currents of the world run." But all of this becomes more apparent in James' actual analysis of conversion and mystical experience.

a. Conversion and the Field of Consciousness

When in *The Varieties of Religious Experience* James came to offering a psychological description of conversion, he asked his audience to think of that which most would have called the "soul" as a "field of consciousness."[27] He supposed that Buddhists might find the metaphor congenial. It is a conception closely allied to his earlier notion of consciousness as a stream; and in fact it seems clear that throughout this part of *The Varieties* James was drawing freely on his own psychological theory.[28] If readers do as James requested, then we can recognize that this field is susceptible to change. Indeed, it has something of the nature of a flux, the importance of which will become more apparent shortly. Within each field of consciousness there is a focal point that may be now more and now less energetic or intense. Around such habitual centers of personal energy our transitive feelings of self converge. Here are our overriding ambitions and deepest fears, our loves, ideals and other strongest motives. Our sense of identity and of what belongs to us—or of what we belong to —grows large or small as the energy of the focal point varies, at times being high or "hot" and at times being low or "cold." Our sense of the character which our world has changes in a corresponding way.

The "field of consciousness" has also a margin, which is not so much a definite line as it is an indefinite zone, also subject to change. Our lesser interests and convictions lie in the neighborhood of this zone. James put a strong emphasis on the margin feature of consciousness. "Margin," "threshold," and equivalent terms not only occur frequently in what he wrote about religion, they also appear at important junctures in his descriptive and analytical account. Along with them he also used the word "limen," a synonym for threshold, particularly in the compound word "subliminal." On occasion James also used the word "subconscious," but the contexts make it clear that it is the notion of threshold that was uppermost in his mind; and what he meant to convey was that what lies within and what lies beyond the margin of consciousness are continuous. The difference between these two regions is not a difference in kind but a difference between what falls within awareness or attention and what falls outside. This idea of margin or threshold directs us to an all-important characteristic of consciousness in conversion experience.

In a typical potential religious convert, the accustomed or habitual center of personal energy may be a sickly feeling of worthlessness and moral frailty coupled with a corresponding sense of the world as bleak and repugnant. The words that escaped from the mouth of the prophet Isaiah in the temple may be taken as representative of the thoughts of untold numbers of such persons: "Woe is me! For I am lost; for I am a man of unclean lips, and I dwell in the midst of a people of unclean lips." But in the neighborhood of the margin zone lies a longing to be identified with the powers that make for the world's salvation, a yearning to be counted righteous. James made allowance for religious conversions in which the individual cooperates with the processes of change of mind by willing a change. But such volitional conversions are less dramatic and less significant than the kind in which no effort of will can exchange the habitual center of personal energy for the yearnings that linger near the margin.

The most straightforward way in which to describe conversion as a psychological event is to say that there occurs a sudden transposition—with which the conscious will has apparently nothing to do—of the former habitual center of personal energy and one of the yearnings lodged near the marginal zone. When this transposition takes place the subject becomes a re-organized field of consciousness. An old sense of self gives way to a new. According to the traditional Christian language about such events, the individual has been born a second time. Often this re-birth shows a vastly widened field of consciousness with a new center of interest and a deeply altered sense of the world. The testimony of David Brainerd, an 18th-century missionary to the American Indians, reflects these features. After agonizing over his lost condition in many painful hours of prayer, Brainerd experienced a radical change, and he described his new state in the following way:[29]

My soul was so captivated and delighted with . . . God that I was even swallowed up in him [and I] had no thought about my own salvation, and scarce reflected that there was such a creature as myself . . . . I felt myself in a new world, and everything about me appeared with a different aspect from what it was wont to do.

While discussing conversion in these terms James made a suggestion, almost in passing, that offers us further insight into his thinking. He briefly substituted the metaphor "wave of consciousness" for his customary comparison of consciousness to a field.[30] His intention was in part to emphasize the successiveness of our mental and spiritual states—they follow on each other as wave after wave—and in part to pictorialize consciousness as being changeable, now like a steep and narrow wave and now like one broad and shallow. He elaborated this "picture" in an essay, published near the end of his life, reporting certain mystic-like experiences of his own.[31] When the wave is high and steep we do not see that its "foot" slopes away in all directions, because the "subliminal" region is concealed by the surface of the ocean. However, if we envision a wave on an unusually flat and gently sloping beach when the tide is going out, we see the threshold "falling," as it were, "and vast tracts usually covered are then revealed to view." James believed that in a similar way the threshold of consciousness can fall, and when it does a "larger panorama . . . fills the mind with exhilaration and sense of power."[32] According to this way of presenting consciousness, then, conversion would occur when the threshold falls or the margin of consciousness abruptly expands and sensations, memories, and feelings that had before been extra-marginal now flood into consciousness.

Originally James had meant to offer a longer connected account of his own theory of religion in the second half of his Gifford Lectures. In fact the book turned out differently, and only at the very end did James make a sustained, brief commentary on the nature of religion considered philosophically. Nevertheless we cannot overlook the other occasional departures into theory that James did allow himself. One of these takes place in his interpretation of conversion by the image of the changing threshold or margin. Conversion, we have already learned from James, involves a radical disturbance of the prevailing relations between the habitual center of personal energy and the margin-zone of consciousness. Subjects of such experience have often described what befell them as being like the enjoyment of a new sense or a new perception. Jonathan Edwards employed language of just that kind in his *Treatise Concerning Religious Affections*, with which James was familiar and to which he referred. Edwards, whose own conversion had brought him direct acquaintance with the "new spiritual sense" and "new kind of perception" that he sought to describe in his treatise, believed that a new "principle" or "whole nature different from any former sensation" must be at work in such sense awareness.[33] James could not agree with the strong theological implications Edwards drew from the fact of these different sensations, but he found Edwards' description of the saint's altered condition subtle and rewarding. Indeed, in contrast to his general attitude toward theology, James acknowledged "the admirable congruity of Protestant theology with the structure of the mind as shown in such [conversion] experiences."[34] And he further conjectured that there need be no contradiction between the principle of a subliminal or transmarginal consciousness as he used it and the theological notion of the direct presence of spirit in such conversion episodes.[35]

> Just as our primary wide-awake consciousness throws open our sense to the touch of things material, so it is logically conceivable that *if there be* higher spiritual agencies that can directly touch us, the psychological condition of their doing so *might be* our possession of a subconscious region which alone should yield access to them. The hubbub of the waking life might close a door which in the dreamy Subliminal might remain ajar or open. . . . Thus that perception of external control which is so essential a feature in conversion might, in some cases at any rate, be interpreted as the orthodox interpret it.

From the mere length of James' treatment of conversion and of all the circumstances attending it as well as his psychological anatomy of the experience, readers may fairly conclude that not only was the conversion phenomenon itself singularly important to James but also the notion so central to his analysis: the notion of the variable threshold of consciousness or the margin of consciousness that can expand to include what hitherto had inhabited oblivion.

b. Mysticism and the Wider Self

Conversion exerted a magnetic attraction on James, and it yielded much of significance to his interrogation. However, it was only one station on the longer line of his inquiry into religious experience. A pause here to survey the whole path of this line can assist us in following James along the remainder of his way.

After a preliminary circumscription of the characteristics of religion, James first addressed himself to the testimony of those whom he called the "healthy-minded," persons who had experienced no shattering spiritual crisis but had steadily "fought the good fight" with stout hearts and little complaint. While he could not wholly reconcile the differing theological tendencies of these resolute spirits, he judged their testimonies on the whole to manifest an attitude toward the real world as pluralistic. Pluralism, as James explained, does not require of the universe that it be a rational whole but permits evil to stand as an independent, irrational fact and correspondingly permits God or the divine to be less than all-powerful. James' sympathy with such "healthy-minded" persons was unmistakable.

Thereafter, he dealt at length with conversion, progressing from the examination of the "sick soul," the soul sinking under the weight of guilt, to the careful consideration of "the divided self," which meant for him the self stretched out between remorse and unstable assurances of salvation. Conversion constituted the experienced resolution of this sickness and dividedness. From that point James proceeded to examine "saintliness," the condition of those who have laid firmer hold on quietness and confidence and deafened their ears to the voices of doubt. Saints have a characteristic James also admired of carelessness of self, arising evidently from a conviction, "not merely intellectual but sensible," of belonging to "a wider life than that of this world's selfish interests."[36] The mystic state made the last stage of James' exploratory journey through the varieties of religious experience. Mysticism appears, then, to be the goal of his whole undertaking. Nevertheless, it posed particular problems for him.

James approached mysticism with the conceptual tools he had developed and employed earlier, particularly in his discussion of the conversion complex. The most important of these was his notion of consciousness as a field with its variable margin or threshold. But in addition, James made his approach out of a growing conviction of the signal importance of mystical states for the interpretation of religion as a whole. In the letter already cited, written to Henry Rankin during the summer between the halves of the Gifford Lecture series, James went on to state[37]:

In these lectures the ground I am taking is this: The mother sea and fountain-head of all religions lie in the mystical experiences of the individual, taking the word mystical in a very wide sense. All theologies and all ecclesiasticisms are secondary growths superimposed; and the experiences make such flexible combinations with the intellectual possessions of their subjects, that one may almost say that they have no proper *intellectual* deliverance of their own, but belong to a region deeper, and more vital and practical, than that which the intellect inhabits. For this they are also indestructible by intellectual arguments and criticisms.

This passage contains much that is pertinent but we will concentrate on three points. 1) The first of them is that it is evident that to James' way of thinking mystical experience lies on a continuum with conversion and saintliness. The metaphors "mother sea and fountain-head" are telltale. The conversion experience, James had hypothesized, occurs when the threshold of the field of consciousness falls below its customary level and transmarginal energies ordinarily outside the zone of awareness flow in, reorganizing consciousness and establishing a new center of personal energy. The distinguishing characteristic of the mystical experience is that it affords a much more expansive communion of self with that which lies beyond its ordinary margins. The "narrow self" undergoes a rapturous enlargement and illumination. James observed that[38]:

> The keynote of the [experience] is invariably a reconciliation. It is as if the opposites of the world, whose contradictoriness and conflict make up all difficulties and troubles, were melted into one.

The mystic moment may also entail a greatly strengthened sense of unification between *present* sensation and perception and *remote* memories, emotions and perceptions of relations and the like, which are beyond the scope of ordinary consciousness. The mystic takes possession, as it were, of "an extended subliminal self." Sometimes James spoke as though the margin of consciousness were a membrane through which "messages" from the "wider self" pass. At other times he suggested that the "threshold" of "the wave of consciousness" was lowered. But in any case, the manner in which the mystic experiences such enhanced relatedness is not through conception but through intuition and feeling, through a kind of sense perception. Hence, the subject is not newly aware of objects taken singly or discretely but is rather overwhelmed by the "sense of a tremendous *muchness* suddenly revealed."[39]

2) The second point in this letter to Rankin of which we need to take particular note is James' judgment that there is no intellectual expression properly suited to the nature of the mystical state. Hence, the true quality of the experience cannot come to public birth. Therefore, the authority of such experience can extend no farther than the mystic's own life, though others may be aroused to the possibility of such experience by the example of notable religious adepts, the people whom James called "patternsetters." On the other hand, such experiences have an immediate authority for the persons undergoing them, an authority of the kind associated with direct sensation.[40]

> Our senses ... have assured us of certain states of fact; but mystical experiences are as direct perceptions of fact for those who have them as any sensations ever were for us. The records show that even though the five senses be in abeyance in them, they are absolutely sensational in their epistemological quality, if I may be pardoned the barbarous expression—that is, they are face to face presentations of what seems immediately to exist.

Hence mysticism, with its sensational, intuitive character, exhibits in an extreme manner a truth that holds of firsthand religion in general: it carries in itself a certitude analogous to that of our perceptions; but that certitude cannot be transferred from one individual to another. Each person must live it alone.

3) A third matter to take up from James' letter to Rankin emerges from the water imagery he invoked in his "mother sea and fountain-head" metaphors. The suggestion is that mysticism points, insofar as it can be said to "point" at all, in the direction of pantheism and monism. James freely acknowledged this fact.[41] Nevertheless this directedness of mysticism toward a philosophical theology of the Absolute runs counter to the practical implications that James thought he discerned in other kinds of religious experience, particularly in those that admitted the irrational reality of evil. It also went against the grain of James' own personal preference for the attitude that recognizes the universe as a pluralistic universe.

Consequently, when James came to the end of his inquiry and proposed to offer his philosophical conclusions about the nature of religion, the metaphysical status of religious experience, he faced a dilemma. The dilemma presented itself to him as arising out of the incompatible intellectual suggestions that different kinds of religious experience prompted. On the one hand, there was the ample evidence that religious men and women so acted as to make clear that for them not only natural evil but also moral evil and spiritual loss were so real that a perfected universe or an absolute God could not be reconciled with their experience. On the other hand, there was the undeniable testimony as well as attitude of the mystic. A conflict of this order might have persuaded some interpreters to decline to attribute further significance to the matter and to remain simply sceptical or silent. James, however, had made it a principle of his whole undertaking that religious fact, so long as it satisfied his criteria, should be treated as no less real than any other insistent evidence. He disdained every from of dogmatic reduction or dismissal of religion that sought to set it aside on the grounds that it had a neurological or biological origin or that its evidence did not meet the standards of impersonal public science.[42] His inquiry had convinced him that his subject matter was real, and he had furthermore declared that "the life of [religion] as a whole is mankind's most important function."[43]

James' solution to his dilemma, for the time being at least, was to leave in suspension the issue of the Absolute versus the Pluralistic Universe. Religious experience, he cautioned, even the experience of the mystic, is not eternally wedded to any theory of the cosmos. What can be affirmed, James concluded, is that "the conscious person is continuous with a wider self through which saving experiences come."[44] In one of the letters written at the time he was delivering the lectures James went on to say that the farther margin of the wider self "can be treated as by Transcendental Idealism, as an Absolute mind with a part of which we coalesce, or by Christian theology, as a distinct deity acting on us. Something, not our immediate self, does act in our life!"[45] James' flexibility on the point may seem puzzling; however, it was characteristic of him and of his pragmatic method not to pursue issues of speculative interest only and without a practical bearing on life. Moreover, James thought a certain latitude, "a certain freedom to indulge in imagination about [such matters]" to be healthy. We have need to exercise a "certain amount of 'other worldly' fancy," he advised. "Otherwise you have mere morality, or 'taste.'"⁴⁶ But when we add up all that James had to say on the relative merits of the Absolute and of the Pluralistic or Unfinished Universe, there can be no doubt left in our minds that the reality of evil would forever prevent James from joining the ranks of thoroughgoing philosophical idealists or the proponents of the idea of God as perfect, omnipotent and unchanging.

5. Conclusion

We can now draw together the elements we have distinguished in *The Varieties of Religious Experience* and make up an outline of James' metaphysics of religious experience in the following statements:

i) James held that religious experience presents us with full or solid facts, with real facts that we cannot ignore. The "margins" defining what we customarily regard as our real selves are variable. He found much use for the term "threshold" and compound words involving its equivalent, "limen." The deep experiences religious heroes, saints, and mystics report, of which James felt some echo in himself, indicate that the threshold of the steep, narrow wave of consciousness subsides. At such moments a "wider self" floods across the margin-zones that circumscribed our former fields of awareness and encompasses us within a larger system of energy. It is our transitive feelings, the "flights" in our stream of consciousness, occurring in the least visible dimensions of our individuality, which provide the means of access to this wider self.

ii) The wider self of which James spoke is not the God of traditional western theology, although we can discern in it the foreshadowing of the God that process theology presents in our own times. In general, James was reluctant to say much about this deity which acts on and within us effecting conversions and mystical experiences. But that it has the character of "self" appears quite certain. In later life, after the Gifford Lectures, James returned in his philosophical reflections to ponder these matters, and still using the same kind of language, he observed:[47]

Every bit of us at every moment is part and parcel of a wider self, it quivers along various radii like the wind-rose on a compass, and the actual in it is continuously one with possibles not yet in our present sight. And just as we are co-conscious with our own momentary margin, may not we ourselves form the margin of some more really central self in things which is co-conscious with the whole of us?

Nevertheless, James was careful to add that this central self, on whose margins we lie, must also have an "external environment."[48] James was careful, in other words, to preserve his theological pluralism.

iii) Such a deity is not the God of the philosophers, at least not the God of the philosophers of whom James took notice, but rather the God attested by religious experience. James said that the deities in which we actually place our trust are the deities we *use* or *can use*. And that criterion prompts us, according to James, to look not to a God who is perfectly absolute but a God present "in the dust of our human trials."

James provided something like a credo summarizing these articles in his book *Pragmatism*, published several years after *The Varieties of Religious Experience*. It resonates with James' whole view of religion and also with the temperament of James' aggressive, individualistic religion itself:[49]

In this real world of sweat and dirt, it seems to me that when a view of things is "noble," that ought to count as a presumption against its truth, and as a philosophical disqualification. The prince of darkness may be a gentleman, as we are told he is, but whatever the God of earth and heaven is, he can surely be no gentleman. His menial services are needed in the dust of human trials, even more than his dignity is needed in the empyrean.

NOTES

1. Letter to Miss Frances R. Morse, April 12, 1900; in *The Letters of William James, in Two Volumes*, ed. Henry James (Boston: The Atlantic Monthly Press, 1920), Vol. II, p. 127. This collection is hereafter cited as *Letters*.
2. *The Varieties of Religious Experience: A Study in Human Nature* (New York: Random House/The Modern Library, no date), Lecture II, p. 27. Since *The Varieties* is published in several different editions, my references will give not only the page but the lecture number as well, to assist readers in locating the citation.
3. *The Varieties*, Lecture II, p. 27.
4. *The Varieties*, Lecture II, p. 31f.
5. *The Varieties*, Lecture II, p. 131.
6. *Letters*, Vol. II, p. 209.
7. *The Varieties*, Lecture I, p. 9f.
8. *The Varieties*, Lecture I, p. 8.
9. *The Varieties*, Lecture VI, p. 129.
10. *Pragmatism: A New Name for Some Old Ways of Thinking*, ed. F. Bowers, *The Works of William James*, Vol. I (Cambridge, Massachusetts: Harvard University Press, 1975), p. 141f.
11. H. D. Thoreau, *Walden*, ed. J. L. Shanly (Princeton: Princeton University Press, 1971), p. 9f.
12. "Divinity School Address," in *Selected Essays, Lectures and Poems of Ralph Waldo Emerson*, ed. R. E. Spiller (New York: Washington Square Press, 1970), p. 85.
13. *Selected Essays*, p. 179.
14. *Letters*, Vol. II, p. 149.
15. *The Varieties*, Lecture XVIII, p. 437.
16. *Pragmatism*, p. 21f.
17. *The Varieties*, Lecture XX, p. 492.
18. *Psychology: The Briefer Course* (New York: Harper & Row/Harper Torchbook, 1961), p. 26f.
19. *The Varieties*, Lecture XX, p. 489.
20. *The Varieties*, Lecture XX, p. 489.
21. *The Varieties*, Lecture XX, p. 492.

22. *Letters*, Vol. II, p. 211.
23. *The Varieties*, Lecture II, p. 35.
24. *The Varieties*, Lecture II, p. 47.
25. *The Varieties*, Lecture II, p. 47.
26. *The Varieties*, Lecture II, p. 51. See note 1 above.
27. *The Varieties*, Lecture IX, p. 192.
28. This is evident in Lectures IX and X (both on conversion) especially but also throughout the whole discussion of the "sick soul," the "divided self," and "mysticism."
29. Quoted by James in *The Varieties*, Lecture IX, p. 210.
30. *The Varieties*, Lecture X, p. 226.
31. "A Suggestion about Mysticism," in *Essays in Philosophy*, ed. Frederick Burkhardt, et al., *The Works of William James*, Vol. 5 (Cambridge, Massachusetts: Harvard University Press, 1978), pp. 157ff.
32. "A Suggestion about Mysticism," p. 158.
33. Jonathan Edwards, *A Treatise concerning Religious Affections; The Works of Jonathan Edwards*, Vol. 2 (New Haven: Yale University Press, 1959), p. 205f.
34. *The Varieties*, Lecture X, p. 239.
35. *The Varieties*, Lecture X, p. 237.
36. *The Varieties*, Lecture XI, p. 266.
37. *Letters*, Vol. II, p. 266.
38. *The Varieties*, Lecture XVI, p. 379.
39. "A Suggestion about Mysticism," p. 159.
40. *The Varieties*, Lecture XVII, p. 415.
41. *The Varieties*, Lecture XVII, p. 407ff.
42. *The Varieties*, Lecture I throughout & Lecture XX, p. 491n.
43. *Letters*, Vol. II, p. 127.
44. *The Varieties*, Lecture XX, p. 505.
45. *Letters*, Vol. II, p. 150.
46. *Letters*, Vol. II, p. 214f.
47. *A Pluralistic Universe*, ed. F. Bowers, *The Works of William James*, Vol. 4 (Cambridge, Massachusetts: Harvard University Press, 1977), p. 131.
48. *A Pluralistic Universe*, p. 140.
49. *Pragmatism*, p. 40.

"The Generous Eye"
A Sermon

The light of the body is the eye:
if therefore thine eye be single,
thy whole body shall be full of light.

But if thine eye be evil,
thy whole body shall be full of darkenss.
If therefore the light that is in thee be darkness,
how great is that darkness!
Matthew 6:22-23 (Authorized or
"King James" Version)

Introduction

THIS particular parable is one that has for a long time especially attracted me and also somewhat puzzled me. The sense of the parable depends on the ancient theory that the eye is the window of the soul, the window of one's spirit and inner being. Recently, I came upon an article by the much revered Henry J. Cadbury, a distinguished New Testment scholar and leader among American Quakers or Friends, in which he advances evidence that the word which is rendered as "single" here in the Authorized Version ought in fact to be translated as "generous." If Professor Cadbury is correct, then verse 22 of this sixth chapter of Matthew should read as follows:
>The light of the body is the eye:
>if therefore thine eye be generous,
>thy whole body shall be full of light.

I. Each of us is acquainted with a particular kind of moment: a moment in which the unwary and unprepared eye meets with the unexpected appearace of *worthfullness*, meets with the unannounced arrival in one's world of being that is tranquil yet energetic: of being-over running-with-being. Too many of these moments are ephemeral and vanish forever below the surface of our preoccupied lives; yet each of us continues to carry instances of them, which though they are fleeting in the transaction are long-lasting in the mind.

One passes, for example, between the steep walls of a narrow gorge in the mountains to be surprised by a staircase of running pools of water with moss and fern or bamboo clasping the cracks in the walls of the gorge; or one rounds the corner of a city street to be caught by the presence of the solid dignity of a firmly planted, well weathered church mirrored, repeated and enlarged in the glass walls of a neighboring skyscraper; or one turns one's gaze in a hall or theater to be fixed by the shape and the lines of a life-filled face wholly attentive and responsive to the action on the stage or the music in the chamber.

Poets have the art to make moments such as these open for sharing. For others of us these chance occurrences remain private; and yet they endow the passing of time for each of us with character and substance. They are instantaneous births, microcreations, filling the immediate world with being and light.

William Butler Yeats called them "moments of glad grace." I should like to give them another name as well, calling them "moments of generosity"—not happenings of only "once upon a time" or "in the beginning," but infinitely repeatable moments that are ordinary and also more than ordinary, for they turn the shadowed cave of self into rooms filled with the amplitude of being and light around us.

Looking turns into seeing; seeing turns into perceiving, so that we take hold of what is there. And in perceiving we ourselves are perceived or taken hold of. In filling our eyes, we are filled. These are instants in which our vision is transformed by a creative energy not our own, and our vision becomes single or capacious and generous.

> The light of the body is the eye:
> if therefore thine eye be generous,
> thy whole body shall be full of light.

II. Up to this point I have spoken only of unpremeditated meetings, of accidental and transforming, grace-filled instants of time. However, this text in Matthew is often taken to have an import quite different from the general tenor of the remarks I have made. The parable as a whole, according to this other interpretation, carries its real weight in the second verse, in verse 23:

> But if thine eye be evil,

that is, if "thine eye" be folded, folded upon itself, doubled and duplicitous or insincere,

> thy whole body shall be full of darkness.
> If therefore the light that is in thee be darkness,
> how great is that darkness!

When the weight of the parable falls on this second verse, then the parable as a whole has a minatory character; it is threatening; it is a warning.

If we convert this saying of Jesus from its parabolic form, from its likening of the eye to a lamp and of the body to a room or house that is to be illuminated by that lamp, then we find that we have something very much resembling an exhortation, a commandment, or an injunction: You are accountable for your seeing! You are accountable for the way you see! Take responsibility for your vision! The gospels contain many words bearing on the manner of our seeing. In the 25th chapter of this same Gospel according to Matthew there is a much more elaborate passage about our responsibility for seeing. It is the scene in which the Son of Man is pictured as sitting on his glorious throne with all the nations gathered before him and as saying to those on his left hand:

>Depart from me, ye cursed, into everlasting fire . . .
>For I was an hungred, and ye gave me no meat:
>I was thirsty, and ye gave me no drink:
>I was a stranger, and ye took me not in:
>naked, and ye clothed me not:
>sick, and in prison, and ye visited me not.
>Then shall they also answer him, saying,
>Lord, when saw we thee
>an hungred, or athirst, or a stranger,
>or naked, or sick, or in prison,
>and did not minister unto thee?
>Then shall he answer them, saying,
>Verily, I say unto you,
>Inasmuch as ye did it not to one of the least of these,
>ye did it not to me.

One way to interpret the failure of those whom the Son of Man rebukes is to say of *them*, is to say of *ourselves*—when we ask, When saw we thee an hungred, or athirst, or sick, or in prison, and did not minister unto thee?—that we failed to see clearly, we failed to recognise. Another way to interpret this failure is to say that we did not obey the second of the two great commandments: Thou shalt love thy neighbor as thyself.

Failure in love or charity, however, is of a far greater magnitude than only an act of disobedience to a commandment. It is more than failure *to do* the law. it is failure *to live* the law—one of the deepest laws of our nature, the law of the reciprocal vitality of the eye and the heart, of the eye and love. The failure of love, of ministering to the life in whose midst we are set, is rooted in the failure of vision. The failure of vision, of recognizing life, is rooted in the failure of love.

Hence, the two kinds of failure are not really two but one. The two kinds of failure belong together and come from the fundamental fault of the dissociation of the eye and the heart. So that lack of charity has as its symptom the folded, ungenerous eye; the ungenerous, unrecognizing eye has as its symptom the restricted, unknowing heart. The two make up one moral and spiritual sickliness of our being.

A different—but still an equivalent—way of construing our faltering in living this deep law of our nature is to say that restriction of heart and vison is weakness of imagination, infirmity in our capacity to recognize ourselves in the world about us and to receive that world into ourselves. For the capacity of recognizing and receiving, of going forth and bringing in, is the capacity of acting on the assurance that it is *one* life which transpires in the world about us and in ourselves. This is the capacity of imagination. For it is by our imagination that we greet the life surrounding us and repeat that life in ourselves. Imagination is the union of love and vision. It is our imagination—or the imagination with which we are gifted and graced—that summons us to relate what we see with what we are.

The lessons to be drawn from the parable of the generous and the folded eye and from Matthew's scene of the last judgment are one lesson. "Where there is no vision, the people perish." When we fear that we are perishing, the light that is in us is darkness. "How great is that darkness!"

III. Paul Strand, the American photographer, once spoke in words coming close to the spirit of our parable of the eye and the body when he remarked about his own work: "When you reach the point where you come to the end of seeing—when seeing is only looking—then you've reached the end of the road." Strand's words echo what Henry David Thoreau once wrote in his journal: "How much virtue there is in simply seeing! . . . We are as much as we see."

To see, as Strand and Thoreau suggest, is to engage in action far more comprehensive, more great-minded and great-hearted, than is mere looking. To see is to do more than to reflect what appears, as a mirror reflects what is in front of it. To see, imaginatively, generously, is to bring what we behold to re-birth in ourselves and to bring ourselves to re-birth in what we behold. It is to take part in creation, in the great act of ordering and of expanding our world and ourselves. This much, I believe, is a fact of existence, an irreproachable truth, a law that cannot be suppressed, to which every poet (every Thoreau), every artist (every Paul Strand), and ultimately every being who discovers or looks for his or her moral and religious nature must testify. The creation groans to be reborn in us, just as we need to be reborn in and with our fellow creatures.

It is therefore a matter of great good providence that our forerunners in the quest of abundant life had the wisdom to make the Scriptures of Israel our own Scriptures as well. For in these Scriptures we have an epic vision, an epic seeing, and a living, poetic or imaginative repetition of that vision, to which we are ever able to return and to make our own, as often as we need. I refer to the Book of Psalms as well as to the visions of the prophets: to the songs that celebrate—and so repeat—the majestic work of creating, sustaining, nourishing, animating, and re-ordering the creaturely life that reaches from the waters above the firmament of heaven to the waters and the dry land below the firmament of heaven.

Song amplifies the heart, makes our inner being spacious and capacious, and unfolds our vision. There is an ancient tradition in Christendom that the Psalms of David are the songs Christ. And, indeed, if we judge from the number of times that Jesus' own tongue repeats the strophes of the singer of Jerusalem, then this seems to be a wise and an insightful tradition. We have in these singers choirmasters who teach us also to sing and to expand.

In this poetry imagination is awakened and the eye is endowed with generous life.

> O LORD, how manifold are thy works!
> In wisdom hast thou made them all;
> the earth is full of thy creatures.

. . . . .

>These all look to thee,
>>to give them their food in due season.
>When thou givest them, they gather it up;
>>When thou openest thy hand, they are filled
>>>with good things.
>When thou hidest thy face, they are dismayed;
>>When thou takest away their breath, they die
>>and return to their dust.
>When thou sendest forth thy Spirit, they are created;
>>* * *
>The light of the body is the eye:
>if therefore thine eye be generous,
>thy whole body shall be full of light.

And to this we should add:

>The great body of life to which we belong
>shall be renewed in us as we shall be renewed in it.

www.ingramcontent.com/pod-product-compliance
Lightning Source LLC
Chambersburg PA
CBHW050834160426
43192CB00010B/2022